AF439480

Hidden Treasure

Hidden Treasure
A Journey to the Heart of God

Brian A. Roraff

Scripture taken from the New American Standard Bible Copyright © 1960, 1962, 1963, 1968, 1971, 1972, 1973, 1975, 1977, 1995, 2020 The Lockman Foundation

Hidden Treasure
Copyright © 2023 by Brian A. Roraff

Dedication

To Mary, my beautiful wife of over 41 years. You are the treasure hidden from me for 23 years. Once your amazing beauty was revealed to my heart, my life changed for the better from that moment on. I love you dearly.

To our seven children (one of which is with the Lord through a miscarriage) and eleven grandchildren (and counting???). Isaiah 54:13, "All your sons (children) will be disciples of the Lord." And so you are. God is faithful. I am so proud of all of you. You, your spouses, your children - our grandchildren, enrich our lives in wonderful and amazing ways.

To John and Kathy (aka: "Ug"). The two of you and your children/grandchildren are a joy and great pleasure to Mary and me. We love you very much.

To my mom and dad. I love you very much. Give Jesus a big hug for me. One day, in heaven, we'll have a wonderful reunion. In the meantime, enjoy your rewards and worship heartily. You are so worthy.

To Mary's dad and mom, Bob and Frieda Gray. I loved you as a son. Thank you for accepting me into your family. You too, enjoy your rewards in heaven and worship heartily.

To Kristin Dewane. Thank you so much for your selflessness in editing and overseeing the final manuscript of *Hidden Treasure*. You are a tremendous gift from God.

To Mike and Ruthie. You are so precious to Mary and I. Thank you for your friendship and your help (Mike) in making the final manuscript possible. Your wisdom knows no bounds.

Contents

<u>Introduction</u>

Having taught science for many years in Christian schools, I grew especially fond of the work of Dmitri Mendeleev. His is a simple story to tell, yet profound. Known as "The Father of the Periodic Table", Mendeleev was one of the greatest chemists to ever live. His contribution to the field of chemistry is timeless.

When all his work was completed, you could trace his masterpiece back to two simple steps. First, he organized all of the known elements of his time according to increasing atomic mass. Second, he then placed them in columns according to similar chemical properties. When the dust settled on his meticulous experimentation and note-taking, Mendeleev gave birth, or fathered, what is now known as the periodic table. Or did he?

As my students and I strove to see scientific laws in the light of the Scriptures, one thing became obvious. While the scientific community lauded Mendeleev as a great chemist, God gloriously used him as an archaeologist, unearthing one of the most stunning natural discoveries of his or any other time.

You see, if we adhere to the Genesis account of creation, then we must understand that the elements Mendeleev worked with and placed into a periodic table were all here since "the beginning." It simply took the better part of five thousand years for someone to unearth this table in one of the greatest archaeological digs ever. Mendeleev wasn't so much the Father of the Periodic Table as he was a tool of the Almighty, used to manifest His power, wisdom, orderliness, and glory.

But the point of this book is not about Periodic Tables and elements (those who struggled with high school chemistry will be glad to hear that). The point is to highlight the seeking that is necessary when you go to look for something that is hidden, and the persevering that is necessary to find that hidden treasure.

Mendeleev sought after something precious and he persevered until he found it. I love that. Ask. Seek. Knock. These were the words Jesus would use to stimulate His hearers into action. Three commands with promises to go with them from a faithful God who is not into dangling carrots in front of His Beloved only to cruelly jerk the carrot away. Three commands with promises that are motivation enough for us to persevere until we embrace that for which our hearts long.

Oh, what a journey! A journey of faith. A journey of great peril, yet greater reward. A journey that ends in the arms of One. Yes, One! Won't you join me as we journey together through these pages to find that One for whom our souls long?

<u>**Chapter One**</u>

Proverbs 2:1-5 - "My son, if you will receive my sayings, and treasure my commandments within you, make your ear attentive to wisdom, incline your heart to understanding; for if you cry for discernment, lift your voice for understanding; if you seek her as silver, and search for her as for hidden treasures: then you will discern the fear of the Lord, and discover the knowledge of God."

As our children were growing up, we would play a game with them that eventually became known as "Hidden Treasure." My wife Mary and I would make some popcorn, put it in bowls for the children and then have them go into another room, close the door, and wait for us to hide the bowls. We would hide them in the lampshade, under sofa cushions, in a blanket, under the curio cabinet, anywhere those little eyes would have at least a bit of a challenge to find that for which their taste buds craved.

We would then yell out, "Ready!" They would come charging into the room, eyes wide open, excitedly looking for their hidden treasure. Usually the older ones found a bowl of popcorn first. Then, as we sensed the younger ones getting a bit frustrated, we would nonchalantly either uncover the bowls a bit to make them easier to find or we would play the hot-cold game with them. (For those who are unfamiliar with the hot-cold game, you simply say "cold" if the person is far from a bowl, and as they move closer you inform them that they are getting warmer, until they get very close, then you yell out "HOT!")

As a father, there were several things I loved about our little game. The anticipation of our children as they waited for Mommy and Daddy to hide the bowls was almost unbearable.

"Daddy, are you done yet?"

"Not yet."

"How about now?"

"Just a minute."

"Hurry up!"

"Okay, now we're ready."

Finally released, those excited eyes and happy feet were enough to make any parent giggle. The shout, "Found one!" brought rejoicing. The inability to find a bowl added a dash of tenderness to the parental heart. And when all was said and done, to hear them say, "Let's play Hidden Treasure again!" oh the satisfaction! The goal had been achieved. That little statement told me that in their estimation, the process…er…the "game", of seeking, was fun, even if sometimes there was a bit of frustration mixed in with the excitement. If they kept their eyes on the prize and persevered, the rewards were great.

The womb out of which our game, Hidden Treasure, was born, was Proverbs 2:1-5. Listen to the verbs sprinkled throughout the first four verses: *receive, treasure, make, incline, cry, lift, seek, and search.*

Read those words again and meditate on them for a moment. One can almost sense one's spirit being raised up into a heavenly, holy, communion with Someone.

I have found that the original Hebrew words expand and sometimes even completely change our paradigm of the truths being conveyed in the Scriptures. For instance, "receive" means "to take". This is not simply a passive word. There is action involved.

"Treasure" means "to hide by covering over". There is an implication of hoarding (isn't that an evil word?) and protecting something. Those sound like spiritual warfare words. Why would you cover, hoard, and protect something unless there was potential for a thief to come who had the purpose of stealing and plundering?

"Make" means "to prick up" the ears. There is an attentiveness, an alertness needed. We need to have high expectations, believing something's going to happen. There is going to be an encounter! Hallelujah! A soldier standing at attention (pricked up, so to speak) knows two things are certain: he will eventually get a command, and when he gets the word, he must obey.

"Incline" means "to stretch or spread out". We are encouraged to involve ourselves in stretching, reaching, longing, yearning, hungering, and thirsting. What a glorious invitation! What a vigorously refreshing exercise!

"Cry" means "to call out". It is related to a word that means "to encounter through the idea of accosting a person that you meet". This idea brings forth an interesting concept. Normally, if we cry out for someone, we have a mindset that they are a great distance from us. We may possibly even feel that they are unreachable. There is almost a sense of hopelessness that can attach itself to us as we "cry out".

However, we find in the Hebrew that this word actually means "encountering someone through the idea of accosting them". Accost is a very intimate word. According to Webster's dictionary, it means "to bring side by side in order to speak to someone". The main word in accost is the Latin "cost", which means "rib". Now, let me ask you, what did God take from Adam to form Eve? What was their relationship, if not intimate?

Cry out! He is your Bridegroom! He is not unreachable. Let hope live in your heart once again. He is near!!

"Lift" means "to give". Selflessly. No more pity parties. It is time to re-channel that energy lost in fruitless sulking. Redirect that energy toward giving yourself to the One who first gave Himself to you. He is surrounding you with His love *(Psalm 32:10).*

"Seek" means "to search out (specifically in worship or prayer)". There is an implication to the word which requires one to "strive after". When you strive after something, there will always be great, earnest exertion involved. Blood, sweat, and tears, they used to call it. Straining. Paul said, "That I may be found in Him," and, "That I may know Him," *(Philippians 4:9, 10).*

"Press on toward the goal!" (Philippians 4:14)

"Search" means "to seek". It is a word that is used in cause and effect relationships. Someone or something is concealed or hidden and someone else receives the invitation to search for it. I love the way our Father plays hide-n-seek. He is always the one who hides behind the tree with one leg or arm sticking out. He seems to always drop a map into our hearts which leads to the hidden treasure. It is almost like he actually wants to be found or something! Go figure!

When, in *Proverbs 2:1-4*, we add the objects to these eight verbs; sinews, flesh, and skin (*Ezekiel 37:6*) begin to grow on the skeletal sketch of what God is encouraging us to do.

"Receive My sayings"
"Treasure My commandments"
"Make your ear attentive"
"Incline your heart"
"Cry for discernment"
"Lift your voice"
"Seek her as silver"
"Search for her as for hidden treasure".

There is an intensity to this thing. We begin to get a taste of the drawing power of the One who said, "No one can come to Me unless the Father draw him," (*John 6:44*), and again, "You did not choose Me, but I chose you," (*John 15:16*).

There is one small word that needs to be brought to our attention at this time. Did you see it as you read verses 1-5? If you missed it, I understand why. Like I said, it is small, only two letters. There it is in verses 1, 3, and 4 and implied many more times. It is the word *if.*

Did you also notice how verse 5 begins? "Then". Now, just a few reminders on "if-then" relationships. If you do the "if", then you get the "then". If you don't do the "if", then you don't get the "then". The only way you get the "then" is if you do the "if"!!

Paul, in the Areopagus at Athens, said it like this, "That they (every nation of mankind) should seek God, if perhaps they might grope for Him and find Him, though He is not far from each one of us." (*Acts 17:27*).

Amazing how God puts conditions on His unconditional love. Two hearts: one divine, one human. One drawing, one being drawn. One desiring intimacy, one not sure what it wants… until it finds it, and THEN? Divine love imparted. Unconditionally. Forgiveness given. No strings attached.

I've noticed that the way I usually decide to do the "ifs" in my life is if the "then's" seem to be worthwhile. I mean, let's be real. The "ifs" are a lot of work: make, incline, cry, lift, seek… The "then" had better be worth it! So, I find I have to count the cost. Is it worth getting out of bed a bit earlier? Staying up a bit later? Giving up something I love to do?

"Then you will discern the fear of the Lord, and discover the knowledge of God," (*Proverbs 2:5*).

"...that they should seek God, if perhaps they might grope FOR HIM AND FIND HIM," (*Acts 17:27*). (Emphasis mine.)

"O dry bones, hear the word of the Lord. Thus says the Lord God to these bones, 'Behold, I will cause breath to enter you that you may make flesh grow back on you, cover you with skin, and put breath in you that you may come alive; AND YOU WILL KNOW THAT I AM THE LORD,'" (*Ezekiel 37:4-6*).

The "then"? Intimacy with our Creator King! Knowing Him! Not merely knowing about Him! Knowing HIM!! Loving HIM!! Receiving love from HIM!! Is the "then" worth doing the "ifs"? Every heart needs to make that decision for themselves. Taste and see.

Oh heavenly Bridegroom, empower us to do the "ifs". You are worthy! You are worthwhile! Forgive our passivity, our indifference, our laziness, our smugness, our complacency. Stir in us once again a holy zeal to know you, love you, and serve you with all our hearts. We cry out, lift up, and search today, believing that You are worthy, and that You are a rewarder of those that diligently see You. (*Hebrews 11:6*).

Daddy! Are you done hiding the popcorn yet?

Chapter Two

Did you ever notice that God has no problem with confronting us with what we believe? He has this bad habit of bringing people and circumstances into our lives that challenge us to get out of our comfort zones.

Like the time my wife was diagnosed with rheumatoid arthritis. It probably wouldn't have been so bad if she'd have been in her eighties or nineties. But at the ripe old age of twenty-seven, I found my bride of four years needing my help to get on and off our sofa, in and out of bed, and to do various other tasks that a person that age simply takes for granted.

Wouldn't you know it, God would have to go and heal her. Sure, we cried out for discernment, lifted up our voices, searched for it like hidden treasure, asked, knocked… But, who would have ever thought He would go and do something like THAT? For *us*? I mean, I wasn't even sure He did that kind of stuff anymore, at least I was taught that He didn't.

Can you see my dilemma? One second my wife can barely move a muscle for fear of the pain involved. The next second she looks like she's auditioning for a physical fitness video. And all this, in front of a husband who cried desperately for Him to heal her, but was more prone to believe God had put an "Out of Business" sign on the door of His healing shop.

What do I do now? Embrace everything I've ever believed and deny the miracle I just witnessed? Or, deny everything I've ever believed and embrace the miracle I've just witnessed. It was my choice.

You know what happens when God rudely confronts you on what you believe? You realize it's time to grow up. No one else will make that decision for you. It's yours to make and it's yours to live with. But if you don't reject the grace being extended to you in that moment, you find yourself unexplainably rejecting what you believed your whole life and embracing the miracle. Then you wake up one day and realize that the miracle is secondary. It's the *Miracle Worker* that's primary. And then, one day you wake up again and realize that even if the *Miracle Worker* withheld the miracle for reasons only He can explain, His grace is sufficient and He is still worthy of all praise and worship.

Anyway, getting back to the point of this chapter: confrontation. One day, when I was in college, a friend of mine handed me a tape and encouraged me to listen to it. I did. I listened and listened and listened. I got extremely uncomfortable and excited at the same time. I had never heard of the artist, Keith Green, yet I knew the songs he sang on this tape were deeply affecting me. I was a pretty spiritual twenty year old, or so I thought. I knew Jesus and loved Him, or so I thought. It was obvious that the Holy Spirit was confronting me about something, but what?

Then one day, I began to understand. Thinking about Keith Green's music and ministry, I began to realize this man had a passion for Jesus Christ that rivaled David's when he cried out, "As the deer pants for the water, so my soul longs after Thee," (*Psalm 42:1*). I didn't have that.

Confrontation time is decision time. I had to figure out what I *did* have. The answer was clear. Knowledge. I knew that I could beat just about anybody in a good old game of Bible Trivia anytime I wanted to. But the Holy Spirit was now confronting me with the thought, "Are you content to know a lot about Me, or would you rather know Me?"

It's the same thought with which God confronted the Israelites in the first chapter of Isaiah. In verse 10, God seems extremely rude and harsh, calling the Israelite leaders "Rulers of Sodom" and the Israelites "People of Gomorrah". Then, in verses 11-15, God begins to enumerate all the terrible things they were doing with which he was not pleased.

Now, if God is going to call a people "Sodom and Gomorrah", you can just imagine what they were doing. But wait. Closer inspection shows us something different than what we might expect. What *were* they doing that upset God so terribly?

Are you ready for this? They were obeying God! Doing exactly what God required of them as passed down through Moses hundreds of years before.

Look at verse eleven: "'What are your multiplied sacrifices to Me?' says the Lord, 'I have had enough of burnt offerings of rams, and the fat of fed cattle. And I take no pleasure in the blood of bulls, lambs, or goats.'" They were sacrificing animals to God. Why? Because God told them to! Oh, I get it. God was mad because they obeyed Him.

Huh?

In verse twelve, they appear before Him (going to church), and He calls it a "trampling of My courts". In verse thirteen, they're giving their tithes and offerings, and He calls it "worthless"; they're offering incense (prayer) and he calls it "an abomination"; and they're going to church some more and He says, "I cannot endure your iniquity." Boy, is this guy hard to please, or what?

In verse fourteen, they don't just go to church on the Sabbath, but also during new moon festivals and appointed feasts (which He, by the way, appointed), and He calls them a "burden" which He "hates".

In verse fifteen, they're praying. (This is getting scandalous!) God says, "I will hide My eyes from you." "I will not listen." Have you ever had a boss like that? Maybe a mom or dad like that? Can't seem to please them no matter how hard you try? What's up with this Guy?

At the age of twenty, I found myself having a one-sided conversation with God that went something like this: "What do you want from me? I go to church. I even go sometimes when it's not even Sunday? I give money. I usher. I sing the songs. I read the Bible. I pray. I have most of the Bible Trivia questions memorized. Give me a break. Leave me alone. What else could You possibly want from me?"

Rudely, He interrupted my one-sided conversation and said, "You." I melted. See, I believed that if I knew a lot about God and did a lot of the stuff He asked me to do, He would be pleased. He chose to confront me with what I believed.

What do I do now? Embrace everything I've ever believed and deny the LOVE I now was experiencing? Or, deny everything I've ever believed and embrace the LOVE that was now empowering me to pant after Him?

Like I said earlier, when God rudely interrupts your life by confronting you with what you believe, you need to make a decision. You need to grow up. I chose to grow up and be like a little child and embrace that LOVE.

Isaiah 1:3 says, "An ox knows its owner, and a donkey its master's manger. But Israel does not know (Me)." (Parenthesis mine) The Israelites of the Bible knew to do all the right things, but they didn't *know Him*.

To know a lot about Him or to know Him.

We all have a decision to make.

By the way, love is not rude. I Corinthians 13:4-5

Chapter Three

Isaiah 50:4 - "The Lord God has given me the tongue of disciples, that I may know how to sustain the weary one with a word. He awakens me morning by morning. He awakens my ear to listen as a disciple."

I remember it well. Waking up in the morning, looking at the alarm clock. There it was again: five - zero - zero. 5:00 a.m. This was getting weird. Why was I waking up morning after morning at 5:00? Not 4:59 or 5:01. 5:00!!

All right, I'll admit it. I'm a bit slow at times, but I can learn. I finally asked God, what's up with this? Isaiah 50 kept rattling around in my head. I decided to read it.

Verse four jumped into my heart and a journey began that day which hasn't yet ended, and by His grace, never will. I found something out in those early days. God has a voice! I guess I never realized that I had subscribed to the idea that God had terminal laryngitis until He canceled my subscription. He awakened my ear to listen as a disciple.

I think God was so excited to have disclosed this reality to me that He kept this thing up for several months. He'd wake me up at 5:00 a.m. every morning. I, too, was excited at my new-found discovery. I'd throw the covers back, jump out of bed, and race to my quiet meeting place. I didn't even bother setting the alarm in those days, so there was no hitting the snooze button. No rolling over. Now, if that isn't grace, I don't know what is.

I knew that this Scripture was prophetically fulfilled in Christ over 700 years after it was first given to Isaiah. I understood when verse five said, "The Lord God has opened my ear; and I was not disobedient, nor did I turn back" that Christ had to listen to His Father whisper some very difficult things into that opened ear.

Such as?

Verse six: Christ was to give His back to the cat-o-nine tails; His cheeks to those who would pull out His beard. He would have to endure humiliation and being spat upon. He had every reason, humanly speaking, to be found disobedient and turn away from the things the Father was speaking into His heart.

However, He declared in verse seven that "The Lord God helps Me", and in verse eight, "He who vindicates Me is near".

As the Holy Spirit quickened these verses in My heart, I knew there would be mornings that I would be tempted to be disobedient or to turn away from the things He was trying to speak to my heart, either because I didn't want to be convicted of sin, or because I didn't want to hear unpleasantries. However, I found it easy to submit myself to the process of listening to and discerning His voice because it was thrilling to have that intimate fellowship with The King. How I cherished those times!

Then one day, several months later, I woke up, jumped out of bed and went to my place of prayer, as was my custom.

Two hours went by. Nothing. Silence. I consoled myself with the thought that this was a fluke. It would be okay. I could wait until tomorrow morning.

The next morning came. 5:00. I ran to my place of

prayer, crying, "Lord, speak to me. Touch my heart. Let me minister to You. Let me know You."

Nothing again. Two more hours of it. Nothing but crickets and yawning.

I began to get worried. I started thinking that there must be sin in my life. Surely, that was it. After all, Psalm 24:3 asks the question, "Who may ascend into the hill of the Lord? Who may stand in His Holy Place?" Verse four answers the question, "He who has clean hands and a pure heart, who has not lifted up his soul to falsehood, and has not sworn deceitfully." And Isaiah 59 talks about our sin and iniquity separating us from God.

Simple logic concluded that there must be sin in my life. My hands must not be clean nor my heart pure. Praise God!! Now I knew what to do.

I began to pray, "Oh God, show me the sin in my life. I want it exposed so I can confess it, be forgiven and purified from all unrighteousness and get back to the intimate relationship we've had on this holy hill."

Any number of things would come to my mind in those moments, all of which I repented of and/or tried to make restitution for. I was excited. I now had a clean slate. Holy hill of the Lord, here I come.

Next morning, 5:00. Run to my study. Two hours later…nothing. The heavens had turned to brass. I couldn't figure out where God had gone. He was playing hide-n-seek and I couldn't find Him. I was like a small child who couldn't find his popcorn that had been hidden: frustrated, teary-eyed, and confused. I wasn't sure I liked this game anymore. I wondered if there was anything tender up there to receive me. It seemed like everything I sent up, be it prayer, praise, worship, whatever, just ricocheted mercilessly, almost mockingly, back down.

This went on for nearly two months. I became a hollow man. My wife would look at me when I got home from teaching at school and say, "Brian, you went through the motions again today, didn't you?" She could tell.

See, when I taught my students at school, going through the motions killed me. I did not want to stand in front of a class and teach information without imparting my heart. I loved pouring out my life to them, the good, the bad, and the ugly. I felt that God could use all of a man's life to help others see the glory of Christ in a weak vessel. But when you've got nothing to give day after day… when you wake up morning after morning as hollow as the day before… when the thing you most desire and fervently search for seems hopelessly hidden…

I remember just before Christmas break a couple of teachers and I were standing in the hallway talking after school. They asked how I was doing. They knew what I was going through because we shared prayer requests each day. I told them, "Not good". I was almost embarrassed to admit that here I was, the principal of the school, and I would go home every day and pray for a snow day. Pretty spiritual, huh? I just couldn't bear the thought of going to school another day and facing my students… hollow.

Then I told them that the more I thought about it, the more I realized that I couldn't win. If I didn't get my snow day, then I would have to go to school and face those students another day as a hollow man. But if I got a snow day, then I'd have to go out and shovel the stuff.

Then, all of a sudden, I seemed to get even more discouraging enlightenment. I realized that if I got my snow day, not only would I have to shovel the dreaded white, intruding flakes, but then, when I was done shoveling, I'd have to go back into the house. Back where my heart was going to go out to Him. I would go to my secret closet of prayer, and I would seek after Him with all my heart and beg Him to talk to me, to be alive to me, be real to me once again… and He would not be there.

On the way home from school that night, I stopped at a cemetery located a couple blocks from our house. It was around 5:00 p.m. when I pulled into the deepest, darkest part of the cemetery, and in the driving rain, I parked and got out of my van. I began walking through the cemetery.

All I could sense were three words rising up from the depths of my spirit. And in the dark, cold, stormy night I cried out, "GOD, NOTHING SUPERFICIAL!!" A resolve came over me. My face was set like flint.

See, I may be a slow learner sometimes, but with some patience I can get it. It took me nearly two months to realize that God, in His deafening silence, was trying to say something to me. He was trying to get my attention. Maybe I should quit my moping and feeling sorry for myself, and once again be still and get to know my God better… on His terms.

It further dawned on me that if I had gone through this for nearly two months, I could take more. I was still alive. Still had a pulse. Still breathing. Dying inside, yes. But if God had sustained me this long, surely He must be after something, and I knew it had to be good, because *He* is good.

I resolved, "I made it this far. Don't You dare take

Your hot, heavy hand off of me now. I want Your best. I want to learn whatever it is You're trying to teach me. If there's sin, break me open, go down to the root, and put the ax to the thing. If there's revelation You desire to impart, open my heart to receive. But promise me one thing God: nothing superficial. Not now. Not ever. Finish it!"

The very next morning, I went to school and in the first class of the morning - a Bible class - I shared with my seventh and eighth graders the story that you have just read plus one more detail. For the first time in my life, a certain word had passed through my mind in the days previous. Suicide. I never would do anything like that, and I told them so. But as that word passed through my mind, the thought came… when I go to my secret closet of prayer, He won't meet with me. But if I die, He'll have to meet with me. He has no choice. He's got to talk to me. He's got to hold me then.

My seventh and eighth graders sat silent, probably wondering, "This is Mr. Roraff? This is the spiritual leader we've come to know and love? This is our teacher? Principal? Friend? What's happening to him?"

(By the way, I wouldn't recommend such transparency with a group of young people. But God's anointing was there to share, and He had given us a very special teacher-student relationship. I sensed all would be safe.)

The bell rang, ending the first period. We got our math books out, left the room and went into an adjacent room for math, all except one girl who I hadn't realized stayed behind until I got done with attendance.

Before I could begin wondering where she was, she walked into the room with her Bible in her hand. This eighth grade girl walked right up to me, opened her Bible, and announced that God had given her a passage for me. She gave me her Bible and asked me to read from Job 23.

"My complaint is still strong today. God's hand is heavy against me, even though I am groaning. I wish I could go to where He lives. I would present my case before Him. I would fill my mouth with arguments. I would know the words of His answer, and I would think about what He would say. He would not come against me with great power. He would really listen to me," (verses 1-6).

I handed the Bible back to this girl and ran out of the room because I didn't want my students to see their principal/teacher melt into a pool of tears in front of them. How does one explain that kind of response to a group of junior high students? To anyone?

I have become content to know that what Paul wrote is true, "Blessed be the God and Father of our Lord Jesus Christ, the Father of mercies and God of all comfort; who comforts us in all our affliction so that we may be able to comfort those who are in any affliction with the comfort with which we ourselves are comforted by God," (2 Corinthians 1:3-4).

Job suffered. I'm suffering. Job found hope. I could find the same hope because hope comes from the same Source. Job endured. I could endure. Job overcame. I could overcome.

That afternoon we had a devotion at school. As was the custom in our school, we had the varying grades taking the lead during the devotional time. As God would have it, it just happened to be the third graders' turn to lead that day.

All the students in grades one through eight gathered in the fellowship hall. I'll never forget it; two third grade girls had worked up a choreographed dance to a song I had never heard before, sung by a Christian artist I had never heard of before. The singer: Benny Hester. The song: "When God Ran".

As I watched, the young girls, starting far apart, began to dance towards each other. Then as I heard the words,

**"The only time I ever saw Him run
Was when He ran to me,
Took me in His arms,
Held my head to His chest,
And said, 'My son's come home again',
Lifted my face,
Wiped the tears from my eyes,
With forgiveness in His voice, He said,
'Son, do you know I still love you?"**

I saw these two little third grade girls embrace.

For the second time that day, less than twenty-four hours after my fervent, "God, nothing superficial" prayer, I was a puddle of tears. Fifty-plus students turned around and saw me, probably wondering, "What's wrong with Mr. Roraff?" To be honest, I wasn't sure what was wrong with me… until the next day.

It was the fourth and fifth graders' turn to lead the afternoon devotions. Their teacher had them get up in front of the whole school and, one by one, share Bible passages the Lord had put on their hearts during the morning Bible class. One student after another shared. Finally, one little boy read his Scripture and something broke in me. I don't remember who the boy was. I don't even remember the Scripture verse.

It was one of those lightning bolt experiences that you never forget, which has the power to transform you forever. See, I had taught for years that God loved you. That His love is unconditional. It doesn't matter what you've done, said or thought. He loves you because God is love. He doesn't have a billy club. If you mess up, He's not going to come after you to hurt you.

All it took was one little boy and two little girls to set my heart right concerning what I had spent years teaching. In the twinkling of an eye, I finally understood that what I had been teaching and preaching for years, I myself did not believe.

Hebrews 4:12 declares that "The Word of God is living and active and sharper than any two-edged sword, and piercing as far as the division of soul and spirit, of both joints and marrow…"

When that boy read the passage the Holy Spirit had illuminated in his heart earlier in the day, instantly my mind went back to the day before, to the Benny Hester song and to the two girls dancing. At that moment, the Lord asked me a simple, yet profound question, "Brian, what did you expect to see and hear?" Instantly I understood that the reason I wept like a baby was because what I heard and saw during that song was not what I *expected* to hear and see.

Replaying their dance in my head, I heard in my mind's ear and saw in my mind's eye what I expected the words to be:

**"I never saw You run until I saw You run toward me,
Point your finger at me and say,
'I am so disappointed in you.
What is your problem?
Come on. Get it together.
You call yourself a Christian? A leader?
Who do you think you are?
You can't even enter into worship.
You're a failure.
Come on. Gird up your loins. Pick yourself up by the
bootstraps.
Be a man.
You are a major disappointment to Me, Brian.'"**

But that's not what I heard.

That's not what I saw.

I was forever undone.

I was forever redone.

"Son, welcome home."

"Oh Daddy, I really am home."

Father, thank you that there's no billy club. Thank you for not holding a grudge against me. Thank you that even though I often disappoint myself, You are not disappointed in me. Thank you for loving me, no matter what. I receive Your love in my precious Jesus' name. Amen.

Chapter Four

"Hear, O Israel! The Lord is our God; the Lord is one!"
(Deuteronomy 6:4)

This particular Scripture is called the "shema" by the Jewish people because of the first word in the Hebrew exhortation, "shema", which in English is translated "hear'. This Hebrew word has an implication of being attentive and obedient. It would almost be the equivalent in the English language for a speaker to say, "Be quiet and listen up!" Almost, I say, because in our culture, after getting people's attention, we so often follow it up by giving information without expecting or demanding obedience. When God, through Moses, however, told the Israelites "shema", He not only expected to get their attention, He expected them to be obedient to His words.

If you're thinking that the information God wanted to give Israel must have been awfully important for Him to get their attention in such a way, you're thinking correctly. After getting their attention, the information God expected them to obey was what Jesus would call the greatest commandment: "You shall love the Lord your God with all your heart and with all your soul and with all you might," (Deut. 6:5).

But before we break down verse five, let's go back to verse four. It's significant that God did not say, "Hear, O Jacob", or "Hear, O Ephraim", or "Hear, O Jerusalem", or "Hear, O Zion". He said, "Hear, O Israel." Why?

Israel is the Hebrew word "Yisrael", which means "Prince with God". Another rendering of the name is "He will rule as God". Jacob received the name after wrestling with God on the eve of meeting his brother, Esau.

Yisrael comes from two Hebrew words: "Sarah" and "Elohim". "Sarah" means "to prevail". It's the picture, in Hebrew, of a prince. In ancient culture, a prince was a warrior, and that warrior was one who prevailed. When he went to war, he went to win. His mission was to fight, to prevail, and to take over. Losing was not an option. Victory was just a matter of time. Sadly, we have lost this picture in our culture, where a prince has been reduced to nothing more than a wealthy man with a title because of a bloodline, a mere figurehead and a reason for gossip-laden tabloids to exist.

But in the Hebrew culture, "Sarah" was an overcomer, a prevailer. And when combined with Elohim, the name for "Almighty God", one would begin to understand that when Israel went out to war, it was not by their might or power, but by God's Spirit that victory was secure.

"Hear, O Israel." God is encouraging them. He's lifting their head. He's reminding them of the bold, courageous ancestral line they came from. I can hear Him say, "You can do it, too!"

"The Lord is our God." The same Lord that Jacob had, you have! The same Lord that transformed a fretful, cowardly Jacob into Israel can do the same for you!

Then God says, "The Lord is one". At this point, our religious mind says that this is unnecessary information. Already knew that. Three-in-one. One-in-three. Trinity. Got it. Let's move on."

But wait. What is God saying here? The Hebrew word translated "one" is "echad". It means "united". When you are united, you are one, are you not? A husband and wife become one. In God's math, one plus one equals one.

So, what's the point? It's this; there is a Father, there is a Son, and there is a Holy Spirit, and they are united. They are in total agreement. There is no discord on this thing.

What thing, you ask? "Love the Lord your God with all your heart, and with all your soul, and with all your might," (Deut.6:5). That's what they're in agreement on. The Father, the Son, and the Holy Spirit agreed that the reason they created mankind in the first place was so that man and woman could enjoy God, so that we human beings could fall hopelessly in love with our Maker.

Now when you analyze the Hebrew word for "love" in this verse, more revelation comes which enables us, as Christians, to gain God's perspective on how He has empowered our hearts. Before having personally studied this word, I thought it meant to show extreme respect, to hold in high esteem, or to give much honor to someone. Though those things are inherent in the word, the primary idea of the Hebrew word "ahab", translated "love", is "affection for".

When I first realized that, I have to admit, my German-Norwegian stoical mindset began to squirm a bit. I began wondering if Webster had the same definition for affection that I had. So I looked it up. Webster says affection means to have a fond attachment, a devotion, emotional feeling. Literally, the emotional realm of love. Webster's definition was mine.

"Hear, O Israel, the Lord is our God, and we, as a Triune God, are totally united and in complete agreement on this command: you will have great affection for Us; you will have a strong emotional attachment to Us; you will emote great feelings for Us. Yes, you will love Us: Father, Jesus Christ the Son, and Holy Spirit."

This commandment is repeated three times in the Gospels. Matthew 22:37, Mark 12:30, and Luke 10:27. Each time, the word for "love" is the Greek word "agape". This word, agape, speaks of a benevolent love, one which desires to help others. It is shown not by doing what the person loved desires, but by doing what the person loved *needs.*

Did God so love (agape) the world that He gave them what they desired? A million dollars? A new car? A nice home? A championship for their favorite sports team?
No. God wasn't in the business of first and foremost giving us what we desired. He gave us what we *needed.* His Son. Jesus the Messiah. A Savior.

So, from John 3:16, we find out that *we* have one great need which *God* set out to meet.

But from Deuteronomy 6:4-5, we find out that *God* has one great need which *we* are commanded to meet.

What? God, the great Creator and Sustainer of the universe has a need which only we can meet?

That's right.

What could God possibly need?

One thing.
What's that?
You.
Me?
That's right, you.
God needs me?
That's right.

For what?
Not for what, for whom?
For whom, then.
HImself.
God needs me for Himself?
Yes.
But, for what?

Isn't it interesting how we as human beings have such a difficult time understanding simple truths? God needing you is such a simple truth, to which we so often subconsciously respond, "For what?" I would like to say, "Why don't you go and ask Him?" Wouldn't that start a journey for someone who is a curious seeker?

Wasn't it Mary "who was listening to the Lord's word, seated at His feet," (Luke 10:39), who received the commendation, "Mary has chosen the good part, which shall not be taken from her." (Luke 10:42).

Mary needed Jesus, Jesus needed Mary. Mary needed to sit at the feet of Jesus, Jesus needed Mary to sit there. Mary needed to hear the voice of Jesus, Jesus needed Mary to hear Him. Mary needed to rest in the presence of Jesus, Jesus needed Mary to rest in Him. Mary needed Jesus and Jesus needed Mary. Two hearts longing. Two hearts panting. One the Initiator. One the Responder. Two hearts beating as one. Two lives blended together. No one is sure where one life stopped and the other began. Glorious Union!!

Jesus needed Mary and Jesus needs you and me for the same reason a man needs his bride. There's a sense of completeness when the two are together, for truly the two have become one. Can the head feel complete if it's not able to commune with the hand? Is the Bridegroom whole if the

Bride is not in fellowship with Him?

Church: He needs you, He desires you, He longs for you. If a person's soul is panting for the Lord as a deer pants for streams of water, guess what? It's only because He has been panting for us first. Is it not true that we get our cues from Him? We love only because He first loved us.

One thing is needed for Him and for you.

Hear, O Yisrael! Hear, O Church! The Lord is our God. And the Lord is united on this one thing as being needful; "Love Me… please. I long for you. I desire you. I am panting after you. I love you."

Signed,

The Lord Your God

<u>**Chapter Five**</u>

The O.J. Simpson case several years ago got quite a bit of national and international attention. Here was a man, faced with very serious charges regarding a terrible tragedy in his family. He hired a lawyer that I'm sure he felt was the best money could buy because his goal was to be vindicated of all charges, thus clearing his name of any wrongdoing. After a lengthy court battle, O.J. was acquitted and set free.

That scenario is played out in our court system hundreds and thousands of times each day. Charges brought. Lawyers hired. Courts in session. Verdicts determined. Men vindicated and set free or found guilty and placed in prison.

Two thousand years ago, this same scenario played itself out on a cosmic scale. One God and Father of all faced serious charges regarding terrible tragedies in His family. Charges of neglect and abandonment, (Daniel 1:1-2, Lamentations 1:3). Charges of abuse, (Lamentations 1:15, 2:1-9). Charges of not caring, (Lamentations 1:16-17). Charges of all manner of wrongdoing against a God who portrayed Himself as loving, patient, and kind. How could a God who is loving allow such things to happen? Isn't He Sovereign? Almighty? Couldn't He stop this? Wonderings turned into charges by undiscerning minds against a God they thought they knew. But, did they?

A lawyer was found. An Intercessor. A Mediator. An Advocate. One who would go between this much maligned Father and His creation and plead a case for truth and justice. One who would accurately portray this Father's heart, demonstrating a perfect balance between wrath and passivity, love and hate, fear and boldness.

So we see this Lawyer in a fit of rage one moment, overturning money tables, making a whip, setting animals free around the synagogue, while in another moment of time, He's holding small children and babies and blessing them. One moment He's kneeling beside a condemned adulteress, offering words of forgiveness and comfort, and another moment He's pointing His finger in the face of men who would bring her to justice and calling them whitewashed tombs.

What is it with this guy? His inconsistency was confusing even to His closest followers. His brash-one-minute, meek-the-next type of temperament was hard to understand. And His rising popularity was becoming an intense source of jealousy.

Not only was the Father on trial for scandalous charges, but soon, the Mediator would be on trial as well, faced with the exact same charges. Imagine. He thinks He's God!!!

Well, the court in this cosmic drama is in session. The verdict will soon be handed down.

But while we wait for the jury to hand in its decision, let's analyze the proceeding. We can't seem to agree on any one thing to condemn this man. But wait a minute. This constant, irritating claim that He is God, thus challenging my self-centered universe, surely is worthy of some sort of punishment. Death you say? A bit harsh, don't you think? On second thought, maybe not. After all, claiming to be God is serious business. Anyway, one good thing about that possible verdict is it would silence once and for all that nagging voice in my head that says there's someone greater than me in this universe.

Finally, the verdict is in. GUILTY! Guilty of thinking He can love the things I hate and hate the things I love. Guilty of showing mercy to those I've already judged of wrongdoing. Guilty of forgiving those I feel should have forgiveness withheld from them.

If they hate the Lawyer, how do you think they feel about His client? If the Lawyer is crucified, what do you think they'd like to do to the One He is representing?

"His blood be on us and on our children." That was their response. Little did they realize that by judging Him guilty, they condemned themselves. No wonder the Lawyer wept so much. The very ones He came to embrace judged *themselves* unworthy, unwilling, and indifferent concerning His love.

But why did this whole scenario have to be played out two thousand years ago?

From the last chapter, we learned that God has one great need: us! He not only wants to have a relationship with us, He wants to commune, to fellowship intimately with us. There's only one problem, and it's also *us*. Ever since Adam and Eve's fall and subsequent hiding from God in the garden, we have taken on that very nature of being afraid of God and hiding from Him rather than running to Him.

We have assumed God to be a mean, self-centered ogre who wants to keep us from having any semblance of fun on this planet. He, on the other hand, has set His face to show us He is not anything like we, in our vain imaginings, have thought Him to be. That's why O.J. Simpson hired a lawyer. To vindicate himself. That's also why God sent His own Lawyer, His Son.

The main difference, however, is that vindication for Himself was not God's primary motive in sending His Son. *Loving us* was His primary motive in sending His Son. *Loving us* was His primary concern. See, He believed that if He was simply Himself as He walked this earth among us, people would see the truth of who He really is, let go of the lies about Him that they may have embraced, and vindication would follow as naturally as water running down a mountainside.

So, He wanted the truth to be revealed. Truth of who He really is. Truth of what He really thinks about us. But truth, especially, so we could be set free to be His, to receive His love, to give His love back to Him and others. So He sent the Lawyer who called Himself "Truth" to us.

There's only one question remaining. What would each individual soul do with Truth once Truth was revealed to their heart?"

Jesus said in John 17:6, "I manifested Your Name to the men who You gave Me out of the world; Yours they were, and You gave them to Me, and they have kept Your Word."

"I manifested Your Name", means Jesus came to reveal the Truth about the Father. What kind of a Father is He, really? The powerful thing about Jesus' ministry is that even though He was a teacher, His lessons weren't merely spoken aloud. His lessons came with demonstration and power.

When He made known the Father's name of Elohim (Almighty God), He calmed the raging sea, the Sea of Galilee, as well as human hearts. It was as if He was saying, "Here is what Elohim looks like as well and the effect He wants to have on your life. When He made known the Father's name of Jehovah Rapha (God our Healer), the blind saw, the lame walked, the deaf could hear. It was as if He was saying, "Here is what compassion looks like." When He manifested the Father's name of Redeemer, He knelt beside the adulteress woman whom everyone else wanted to stone, and won her heart with kindness, gentleness, and forgiveness. It was as if He was saying, "Here is what Redeemer-Forgiver looks like". When He showed the people the Father's name of Jehovah Tsidkenu (God our Righteousness) and stretched out His hands and died, it was as if He was saying, "Here is what Love looks like."

Everywhere He went, Jesus was consumed with the passion of showing people what the Father really looked like. The totality of His teaching style wasn't just having His students take out notebook and pen, write down terms and definitions, and then take a quiz. He *demonstrated* the definitions of God's names, giving evidence of God's true character. The people experienced the reality of God's names so there would be no question as to who this Father He purported to know and was One with really was.

Frank T. Seekins, in his manual, "Hebrew Word Pictures", explains that the original Hebrew language used both a sound and a picture for each letter in their alphabet. This created word pictures which basically are words as we would know them today, but described by pictures. As I've studied this manual, I've been deeply affected by this ancient language. One word I especially want to share with you as we close this chapter is the picture word for "love":

House

"The Spirit"

Leader

These three characters, in the ancient Hebrew mind, spell "love". The first character is a picture of a tent or house, a place where people dwell. The third character is a picture of an oxhead. To the Hebrew mind, this is a symbol of strength or leadership. When the first and third characters are put together, we have the ancient Hebrew word for "Father". "Father" literally means, "the strength in the house", or "the leader in the house". Who is the strength in the house? Daddy. Abba. Papa. The Father is both the leader and strength of the house.

Next, the middle character is a picture of a man standing with his arms raised. It can also be drawn as a window. It carries with it the idea of someone trying to get your attention to "look at" "look through" or "behold" something because he wants to "show" or "reveal" something to you. Now, when you put this character in the middle of the other two, you get the ancient Hebrew word, "love".

Finally, putting it all together, we understand that to the ancient Hebrew mind, the literal meaning of the word "love" is, "THE HEART OF THE FATHER REVEALED." One needs the Holy Spirit to reveal to us the true heart of Daddy.

If you stop for a moment and look closely, you will see it. You will see **Him**. If you look through the window of Jesus Christ and His life and ministry, you will see the

Father. Look. Take your time. Please look. This is God - your heavenly Papa!

Can you see Him?

P.S. If you're reading this, you are obviously alive. That's telling me one thing. Court is still in session for you. You are the judge and the jury. The man on trial? Jesus Christ. The charge? Claiming to be God. Claiming to be the window through whom men and women, boys and girls everywhere can clearly see the WAY to the Father, know the TRUTH about the Father, and receive the LIFE which is found only in the Father. Before you reach your final verdict, may I beg you to…

BEHOLD THE MAN ON THE CROSS - the One with the raised arms?

Can you see Papa God now?

"Give, and it will be given to you; good measure, pressed down, shaken together, running over they will pour it into your lap. For by your standard of measure, it will be measured to you in return." (Luke 6:38)

Here they were, two guys walking from a busy, bustling city, on their way home after an incredible weekend of one event after another. Things were happening so fast it would make anyone's head spin. Then a stranger joins them as if out of nowhere.

When the newcomer asked what they were talking about, they were amazed that He didn't know. What is *anybody* talking about? It's the only possible news worthy of conversation. It's all about Him, "Jesus, the Nazarene, who was a prophet mighty in deed and word in the sight of God and all the people," (Luke 24:19).

Finding a boldness and a comfort level with this stranger, they went on to tell how He had been crucified. Then, just that morning, they had heard reports of women in their group having angelic visitations announcing that Jesus was alive again. But, sad to say, no one had really seen Him to confirm the angel's message, at least, to their knowledge. It was almost more than a person's mind could absorb in a day. Too much information. Too much confusion. Brain freeze without the ice cream.

Then, before they knew it, and just as the stranger began opening up the Scriptures to them, they were home. It was decision time. My, it had been a long day. But wasn't this guy fascinating? But it was an even longer weekend. But aren't our hearts being stirred as He shares Scripture? But I sure am tired. But I could listen to Him all day (and night) long. But, oh well, He looks like He's going to continue on walking to the next town.

Ah, the test.

How hungry are we? Hungry enough to be fed the richest of foods? How thirsty? Thirsty enough to find only that water that gives abundant life? How desperate? Desperate enough to fight through crowds to touch the hem of His garment? Desperate enough to cry out when everyone is telling you to be quiet? Desperate enough to keep bringing your children to Him, wanting Him to bless them when those that are respected tell you not to, that He's too busy; too important for such matters. After all, He's got a universe to manage.

Are you desperate enough to find out the truth for yourself?

Thank God, there was one more "but" left in these disciples. "But they urged Him, saying, 'Stay with us,'" (Luke 24:29). The Greek word for "urged" in this verse literally means "forced". It's true that the violent take the kingdom by force. These men were hungry. Isn't it interesting that they forced this stranger to stay with them, yet they had no clue who He was? All they knew was that He warmed their hearts. They would not let Him go. That's desperate!

That's also the response Jesus was looking for. "Hear, O Israel, the Lord is our God; the Lord is One. We are united about this one thing: We want you to love Us. We want you to show affection for us. We want you to want Us: Father, Jesus Christ the Son, and the Holy Spirit." Remember that?

David Wilkerson, in a message entitled, "Feeding

Christ" (February 13, 2002), writes, "Recently, after my prayer time, I was about to get up and leave. But I heard a still, small voice whisper, 'David, please don't go. Don't leave Me yet. I have so much more to share with you. There's a lot in My heart I wish to show you, about the needs of the world and the condition of My church. You feed Me by listening.'"

Now, there's an amazing concept. We feed God just by listening, by staying in His presence, abiding, not leaving or letting Him leave. These disciples were meeting His needs. Agape-ing Him. Serving Him. Ministering to Him. Loving Him.

It should not surprise us that Christ fed these men, first spiritually, and then physically as He broke bread with them. After all, they were feeding Him. Give and it will be given to you. Hmmm. Selah.

Pastor Wilkerson concludes his article with these observations about the Emmaus disciples: "Thank God, these disciples constrained Jesus to stay. Otherwise, they never would have had their eyes opened to the living Christ. They would have returned to Jerusalem with a dead-letter testimony: 'We met someone on the way to Emmaus who taught us deeply from the Word. It set our hearts on fire, and we understood Christ as never before.' The other disciples would have pressed them asking, 'But did you see the Lord? Did you touch Him? Did you find out where He is? You say your hearts were set on fire. But tell us, is Jesus alive?' Sadly, they wouldn't have been able to answer."

The only question left is this: with what measure do we want Christ to feed us? Shall we settle for crumbs from the Master's table? If so, it should be noted that somewhere along the way, we decided to have the Master settle for crumbs from the servant's quarters. For by your standard of measure it will be measured to you.

Oh Father, increase my capacity to love You. Rid me of the clutter that takes up space in my heart, space that You could be occupying, space in which You, and You alone deserve to dwell. Help me to love You with *all* my heart. Make me a hungry, thirsty, desperate disciple. I love you.

<u>**Chapter Seven**</u>

Teachers teach. Students learn. When the process is complete, it's test time. The test, contrary to popular opinion, is not some strange form of torture or punishment. It is a tool used to find out whether or not the student has learned the material taught. How well the student does can determine whether he or she is ready to move on to other material or whether he needs to be re-taught the same lesson.

I think many students dread test time for varying reasons. God's feelings on the subject, however, are quite different. Rather than dreading tests, He encourages us to "Consider it all joy, when you encounter various trials (experiences, tests), knowing that the testing of your faith produces endurance," (James 1:2-3).

Why the dramatic difference in outlook on test-taking? I believe it all has to do with perspective. For many, when a test comes, we often feel unprepared, possibly overwhelmed, and afraid to fail. Because we lack confidence, anxiety can come in and begin to rule our minds. This brings uncertainty into the process and we find we are not functioning like we know we are capable of.

God, on the other hand, had a very refreshing perspective on tests. He knows we can pass them. Why? Because He's the Teacher. And He's a pretty good one.

But, you say, He may be the Teacher, but I'm the student, and I don't have a lot of confidence in my ability to learn, let alone test-take.

Let me ask you this. Have you ever known a teacher who would stop mid-chapter in a book and immediately give a test on the whole chapter? (By the way, if you do know such a teacher, you may need to forgive that teacher - or maybe repent for your class's behavior that led to it - just a friendly suggestion.) Doesn't a *good* teacher usually finish *all* the material needed to be covered first, and then give a test?

Now, if we agree that God is good, then He must have given us *all* the material we needed before handing out the test. After all, He has given us "Everything we need pertaining to life and godliness," (II Peter 1:3). He also believes that we "Can do all things through Christ who strengthens us," (Philippians 4:13). "He has not given us a spirit of fear, but of power, and love and a sound mind," (II Timothy 1:7). If we don't understand what we've got with this indwelling Christ, that's okay. We'll learn through life's issues as He imparts to us a teachable, pliable heart. He'll teach, then test.

Because He is love, He "Believes all things, hopes all things, endures all things," (I Corinthians 13:7). In other words, He believes in us. He believes we can do it. And if we fail, it's okay, because He is patient, and His hope in us will not fail. He will endure and persevere through all things with us because a good teacher never gives up on his students. He knows they can pass. He just asks that we endure; that we not give up on Him or ourselves.

He knew Abraham could pass His test. Oh, and what a test. Take your son and kill him. The son I promised you. The son for whom you waited twenty-five years. The son of prophecy past as well as prophecy future. The son conceived and born through the will of God. A miracle. The son you love tenderly. Kill him. Now.

Abraham obeyed and was in the process of following through on this unspeakable act when the angel of the Lord intervened and said a very curious thing: "Do not stretch out your hand against the lad, and do nothing to him, *for now I know that you reverence God*, since you have not withheld your son, your only son, from Me," (Genesis 22:12).

I have a hard time believing that an omniscient God didn't know that Abraham reverenced Him. I liken this to God calling to Adam in the garden of Eden, "Where are you?" (Genesis 3:9). God was not looking for information. He knew where Adam was. After the fall, however, *Adam* wasn't sure where Adam was. What was his standing with God now? Was God mad at him? Did God love him anymore? Doubts, fears, and confusion entered Adam's mind for the first time. That's where Adam was. A scary place. God knew that. He needed to confront Adam with the consequences of his sin, while at the same time reassuring Adam of His undying love and devotion to him.

"For now I know that you reverence God." Like I said, I believe God knew Abraham's heart. I believe God knew Abraham loved Him and was wholly devoted to Him. However, God also knew Abraham's heart was desperately wicked (Jeremiah 17:9). So, the key involved helping Abraham come to know something he desperately needed to know, something God already knew.

My guess, knowing a little bit of how Satan works, is that since the conception and birth of Abraham's miracle son, Abraham was probably tormented frequently with thoughts like: "You love Isaac more than God, don't you! You sure spend a lot of time with him, time you used to spend with God. Abraham, Isaac is more important to you than God, isn't he? Why, he's becoming an idol to you. And you keep giving testimony of the miracle birth. But you're really trying to build your own reputation, your own ministry, take credit from God, steal His glory, and bring attention to yourself."

Torment. Anxiety. Doubt. Fear. Wondering. You know the worst thing about questions like that are the wonderings with which they fill our souls. Is it true? Am I in sin? I still love God… I think.

How are the incessant voices silenced? And not just for a brief season. For good. Not just for a time of relief, only to come back a few hours or days later. Forever.

How?

Enter… the test. God knew something about Abraham that Abraham needed to know… again. That nothing could separate Abraham from God's love. Nothing. But wait. Here comes that tormenting thought again: sin could. Sin could separate him from God, after all, "Your iniquities (Abraham) have made a separation between you and your God," (Isaiah 59:2). There are those voices again.

Maybe I have sinned. Maybe I have grieved God's heart. Maybe Isaac is an idol. Maybe I do love him more than God. O God! It's all so confusing. I don't know what the truth is anymore. Help me!!!

May I ask, how did they atone for sin in the Old Testament? That's right; altar sacrifices. "Abraham, take your son, your only son, and…" How that word must have pierced him. He knew the wages of sin. He didn't doubt or deny the word, though, because "My sheep hear My voice, and I know them, and they follow Me," (John 10:2-4). He simply obeyed, because, "If anyone loves Me, he will obey My Word," (John 14:23).

Abraham demonstrated that love is not just a feeling or emotion. There is a higher kind of love that persists even after the feelings stop, even after the feelings and rationalizations seem to shout louder than the voice of God in our souls. It's the love with which God loves us. It's the agape love we talked about in chapter four. It's the love that truly meets God's needs. And as we've mentioned, give and it will be given to you. What measure was Abraham willing to give? So, probably numb and a heartbeat away from pouring out an ocean of tears, Abraham went where he was commanded… with his son.

Isn't it neat how God provided a *Lamb* for Abraham? And in the person of Christ, a lamb for you and for me? Now nothing can separate us from the love of God. Thanks be to God through Jesus Christ our Lord! If God is for us, who can be against us? In all these things we overwhelmingly conquer through Him who loved us (Romans 8:38-39, 7:25, 8:31, 37).

Now, finally, Abraham knew what God knew.

An eternal seed planted in a man, possibly dormant for a season, but now… alive, growing, healthy, and strong. That seed of love weathered a storm of torment, condemnation, and accusation, all voices aimed at separating him from God's love. Now Abraham knew that he did indeed love God with all his heart, soul, and might! *That* was the truth! You see, love is proven by obedient faith. And obedient faith brings a revelation of God's greatness, goodness, and glory.

Some would say it's not important for Abraham to know that he was fulfilling the greatest commandment to love God with all his heart, mind, and strength. The only thing that is important is to know that God loves you.

To those who would subscribe to that ideology, allow

me to ask you a few questions.

What do you do with those nagging, persistent thoughts that accuse you of idolatry? You know, those thoughts that tell you that there's someone or something more important in your life than Jesus. Those thoughts that accuse you of having lost your first love.

Oh, I see. You repent. Good for you. Then let me ask you this: what do you do after you've repented time after time, month after month, year after year, until a decade or two of guilt, condemnation, and repentance cycle themselves through your soul leaving you exhausted, frustrated, and no further in the process of eradicating the voices of accusation from your waking hours than when you started?

I believe it is true that knowing that God loves you is first and foremost. Resting in that love is vital. After all, we only love Him because He first loved us.

However, I believe a significant mark of one's maturity is passing the test of love, our love for Him. To walk through the highs and lows, the victories and defeats of the Christian faith, to persevere when all you can think of is quitting, to be confronted with selfishness and pride and choose crucifixion. To be so close to a dream fulfilled, yes, holding the reality of that dream in your very hands, and being willing to let it go because you find your heart has been captured by Someone more beautiful. To be able to discern the voice that insists you left your first love as not being the voice of God's Spirit, but a poor, counterfeit voice belonging to the enemy. To be able to cry, "I am His, I am my Beloved's," (Song of Songs 7:10), and know it's true because you know your heart is a bond slave to no one else and nothing else.

God's love had conquered Abraham years before. Now a reciprocal love for God had grown in him to such a degree that that realization, through the testings of God, probably amazed even him. Certainly, the angels were staggered.

Chapter Eight

As we begin this chapter, please take note: if you feel that there is more to be had in this life than what you are experiencing, you are right. You are on the right track. Keep going. Don't stop. Don't get distracted. Endurance, or perseverance, is a Godly virtue.

Why else would Paul pray that "You, being rooted and grounded in love, may be able to comprehend with all the saints what is the breadth, and length and height and depth, and to know the love of Christ which surpasses knowledge…" (Ephesians 3:17-19). Paul is saying, "There's more. Go for it." Why settle for a drop or two when there's a whole ocean, no, an infinite universe of God's love to explore and receive.

Oh, "To know the love of Christ." "That I may know Him." "That I may be found in Him." (Ephesians 3:18, Philippians 3:10, 9). Such longing. Such desire. Such determination.

We must understand that knowing Christ has nothing to do with gaining more academic information. That's what Paul meant when he wrote, "To know the love of Christ which surpassed knowledge." I can know a lot about a professional basketball or football player. I can know a lot about the President. I can do research, read books, magazines, articles in newspapers or on the internet, watch the sports or news on television so as to gain much knowledge about the man and *still not know* him. It's not until I actually meet the Man face to face, and then spend time with Him day after day that I will actually begin to know him. This is experiential knowledge, not mere academic knowledge.

But we must also understand that this type of knowledge comes only at a cost. Jesus said, "If anyone wishes to come after Me, he must deny himself, take up his cross, and follow Me," (Mark 16:24). He also said, "...The kingdom of heaven suffers violence, and violent men take it by force," (Matthew 11:12). Another version says, "The kingdom of heaven is forcibly entered, and violent men seize it for themselves."

Let me ask a question: is it possible to truly seize a kingdom without having seized the king? I believe the church in many countries is so terribly anemic and malnourished because we have been deceived into thinking we can seize God's kingdom without apprehending the King. We need to conquer this King Jesus! We need to capture His heart! We need to ravish His very being! I believe God withholds His fullest purposes for us until we become spiritually violent!

That's why I appreciate the example the Emmaus disciples give to us. They demonstrate the violence necessary to conquer the King. They demonstrate the cost that needs to be paid, as flesh wrestles with spirit, in order to receive this revelatory knowledge.

That's also why I appreciate Jacob. In my NASB Bible, the title of Genesis 32 is "Jacob's Fear of Esau." In understanding what Jacob went through as recorded in chapters 32 and 33, we need to understand that God will, at varying points in time, confront us on our greatest weaknesses.

One of my greatest "weaknesses" is selfishness, especially when fatigued. If I had been one of the Emmaus disciples, I probably would not have been the one to invite Jesus in. In fact, if my buddy had given a hint of inviting Jesus in, I probably would have taken him by the elbow, walking him away from Jesus a few steps, and, under my breath, told him, "Are you kidding, I'm exhausted. Don't invite him in. Let him go. Maybe we'll run into Him again sometime, someplace, and we can get the rest of the story then. Not now, though. I'm too tired." That, my friends, is the same flesh that Peter, James, and John exhibited in Gethsemane, when they were too tired to stay awake with Jesus. Remember? The spirit is willing. The flesh is weak. Which will win?

I don't know the answer to that question on any given occasion. But I do know this: the flesh will win every time until the spirit begins to arise within us, and awakened by the Holy Spirit and His power, violently destroy the work of the flesh, and seize both King and Kingdom.

Jacob had a great weakness. Fear. His brother, Esau, had wanted to kill him for the last twenty years. Jacob, in fear, ran away and spent the last two decades with his uncle Laban. Two wives, two concubines, and twelve children later, Jacob comes back home.

On the way, suddenly a terrifying thought seizes him. He's coming back to a brother who, if still alive, wants to kill him. And that's no exaggeration.

It's in this gripping reality that we pick up Jacob's story in Genesis 32:24. "Then Jacob was left alone, and a man wrestled with him until daybreak." That man, I believe, was Jesus. God incarnate wrestled with him.

"And when He saw that He had not prevailed against him…" (Verse 25). If you remember from chapter four "sarah" means "to prevail". Israel, which would become Jacob's new name through this encounter, means "one who prevails and overcomes with God". Jacob was not going to quit this intense struggle in prayer which outwardly looked like a wrestling match. Jacob had determined that God, who was playing hard to catch, was not going to prevail against him. He would not let God go. *He* would be the overcomer. His flesh would not win. The man with whom he was wrestling in prayer held the key, and somehow, some way, he was going to get it from Him so he would no longer be in bondage to fear.

"And when He saw that He had not prevailed against him, He touched the socket of his thigh; so the socket of Jacob's thigh was dislocated while he wrestled with Him," (verse 25).

"Then He (Jesus) said, 'Let me go, for the dawn is breaking,'" (verse 26).

When I put myself in Jacob's shoes, I wonder what I would have done then. Jacob wrestled all night in prayer with God. He was in pain. Then, just as the dawn is breaking, God tells him, "That's enough, Jacob. That was an excellent prayer time. Whew!! I'm sure you are worn out. I AM. Well done, good and faithful Jacob. I will lift My presence from you now and we'll just call it a great prayer meeting. You can let me go now."

I bet Jacob had a flood of thoughts running through his mind? "Yeah, You're right. That *was* a great prayer time. Wow. I completely lost track of time. Didn't realize it was so late. Sorry to keep You so long. Can't wait to give this testimony in church! Will they be impressed by how spiritual I am! Let You go? Let Your manifest presence lift from me? Well, I guess I never realized just how tired I really am. Let You go? Well…"

"I will **not** let You go until You bless me," (verse 26).

(Emphasis mine.) That, my friends, is a violent man forcibly seizing the King and the Kingdom for himself. That is a man who will take the test of God and pass it. That is a man who prevails against God, Who supposedly wants to leave, but in reality, overcomes with God against his own flesh.

Oh, and what flesh Jacob needed to overcome. I'm not sure he knew what was coming next, because it's at this point that the Lord confronts Jacob at his greatest weakness. We find out that it wasn't fear after all that was Jacob's Achilles heel. There was an identity issue Jacob needed to settle once and for all.

"So He said to Him, 'What is your name?'" (Verse 27).

First, Jacob gets his thigh dislocated. If you've ever had an appendage dislocated before, you'll never want it to happen again. Guaranteed. Incredible pain. Then, the test of responding to the request to let the Lord go. Then the realization of the lateness of the hour and the fatigue factor.

But none of those tests, I believe, compared to this final exam. What is your name? What is my name? Really? After wrestling all night with me, that's all you got? That's your parting question to me? Seriously? Again, legions of thought must have raced through Jacob's mind. "Ask me anything. Is the sky blue? Do fish swim? Ask me anything. Just don't ask me that!"

Jacob was all of a sudden confronted with the reality of an answer that needed to be uncovered which he knew deep in his heart was true but always fell short of wholeheartedly admitting. There was always an excuse. Always an alibi. Always someone else to blame.

But no more. Walking away from truth now seemed unthinkable. He was embracing the embodiment of Truth. Truth had dislocated his thigh and he wrestled on. Truth had just asked him to let Him go and he refused. Truth had now asked him what his name was. Courage needed to be found to answer that question truthfully.

Startling realizations set in. If I let go of the Truth now, what do I have left to hold onto? The hollowness of lies and deception was the stinging answer that dawned upon his consciousness as surely as the sun was dawning on a new day. Truth and light were being imparted and love and forgiveness was being released.

"What is your name?"

Was it truly going to be a new day for Jacob, or was it just going to be the same old fears, the same old lies, the same old torture, the same old oppression?

"What is your name?"

Through sweat and tears, I can hear Jacob sob his answer, "My name is Jacob. Deceiver. I am a deceiver. It's true. I've been running and running for twenty years, scared to death of my brother Esau. I deceived him twice. I am a supplanter. A heel-holder. It's true. Why did you have to ask me what my name is? It's Jacob!!!"

Ah, the cries of a man's soul under the conviction of the Holy Spirit. Cries of bonds breaking, chains falling off. Tears of healing, washing away decades, yes, a lifetime of deception. Then cries of joy at the finding of freedom.

Face in the dirt. Tears creating mud. Hands still clinging to Truth, elusive Truth, of whom he would not let go.

Cruel, you say? Was God cruel in asking Jacob his name? No. You see, God's in the healing business. He *had* to confront Jacob. And Jacob was just desperate enough to let God confront him and to come forth with a true answer.

"And He said, 'Your name shall no longer be Jacob, but Israel, for you have striven with God and with men and have prevailed,'" (verse 28).

You're no longer the deceiver, the supplanter, Jacob. Why did Christ tell him that? Because he wanted Jacob to know that he was forgiven and that his sin was being removed from him as far as the east is from the west. No more torment. No more condemnation. The old had truly passed away (Jacob); the new had come (Israel).

You are Israel. You are a Prince. A prevailer. An overcomer with God. You have a new identity.

Did Jacob conquer the King or did the King conquer Jacob? The answer?

Yes.

When we feed Christ, when we refuse to let Him go, we overcome Him, yes, we conquer Him as surely as a Bride overcomes her Bridegroom on their wedding night.

Come into our house. Tarry a little longer, stranger. Your words, Your presence is making our hearts burn.

Let me sit at Your feet. I will listen. I will learn. I will understand as Mary did.

Experience Him. Feed Him. This is communion.

May I ask you: do you think Mary would have gotten the commendations she received from Jesus if she would have given in to the pressure her sister was trying to put on her regarding what "real" service to Jesus looked like? Do you think the Emmaus disciples would have been empowered by the revelation of the risen Christ if they had not invited Him into their home to tarry a little longer?

Do you think Jacob would have gotten the miraculous revelation and blessing he received if he would have let his wrestling partner go upon request? If he would have let the pain of the dislocated hip distract him? If he would have let fatigue conquer him at the breaking of a new day? If he would have let self-preservation and pride triumph when asked his name? He asked for a blessing. Boy, did he get blessed, even though it may not have been the way he anticipated.

Father, break me. Break me of complacency and indifference. Break me of excuses and pride. Break me of tendencies toward self-preservation. Papa, heal me. Give me the tenacity to not let You go, whether it's my flesh, the devil, or even You making the request. Give me hunger and thirst for You. Give me passion, passion, and more passion. Thank You for being patient with me. How I love (phileo) You. Give me more love (agape) for You. I choose to feed You today. My heart longs for You. Have Your way with me. You are my God.

Hear, O Israel! The Lord is our god; the Lord is one! You shall love the Lord your God with all your heart and all your soul and all your might.
Deuteronomy 6:4

<u>Chapter 9</u>

Like most boys in middle school and high school, I was growing into independence. Wanting more freedom. Desiring to step out into who I thought I might be. It's sort of thrilling and scary at the same time. You, who have been so dependent for so long on parents or guardians, now see a light illuminating a small, barely legible sign at the end of that long adolescent tunnel that reads: FREEDOM!

Then, one day you wake up and realize that there is at least one obstacle to living in the reality of what that sign promises. For some young people, it may be more than one obstacle. For me, there was one big obstacle to total independence (spelled F-R-E-E-D-O-M). It was my mother. Her controlling, manipulative ways were becoming more and more unbearable with every facial hair the cat could not lick off with milk.

I first became aware of this Jezebelian conspiracy when I was in eighth grade. I was forbidden to ride my bike the two miles to school. Outrageous! Everybody else was riding their bike to school…I think.

Then, at the age of sixteen, I got my driver's license. It was important that I drive a car to school. Everybody else was driving their car to school…I think. Forget that I didn't own a car. Dad had one. Forget that he needed his own car to drive to work. None of that mattered. Don't confuse me with the facts. I needed to drive to school! It's not that I was selfish. It's just that I couldn't figure out why my parents, especially my mom, weren't thinking only about *my* needs and wants.

Did I mention I had a volatile temper? Oh yeah.

Justifiably so, I thought, and I'm sure you would agree. I mean, how unreasonable is it to be trapped in a family that refuses to acknowledge your lordship? Thing is, my temper, 100% of the time, was directed towards my mom. She got the volcanic overflow of Mount Roraff whenever she would not submit to my every whim and fancy.

By the time I turned 25, our relationship was almost irreparably damaged. One day, I remember the Lord confronting me on this. He was pretty blunt. I would need to repent to my mother. If I chose not to, I would be in grave danger of losing my mom. He gave me two options: lose your temper or lose your mother.

Some might think that when confronted with options like this, the decision would be easy. Of course you do not want to lose the relationship with your mother. But for me, it was not that easy of a decision. I had allowed so much bitterness and resentfulness to enter my heart, that it clouded objective truth and any semblance of love.

I wrestled with God's verdict for a short season. Most of the wrestling dealt with the thought that she was the (older) adult - the parent. **She** should approach *me*. She's the one who wronged me. She should start the reconciliation process. On the other hand, what if she never approached me to apologize? What then? Lose temper? Lose mom? Hmmm.

Almost miraculously, the Lord showed me that I still had some semblance of affection for my mother. That revelation secured my decision. I would humble myself, go to my mother, and apologize for the way I treated her during my teenage years. I wondered how it would go. In one last ditch attempt to get out of this humiliating experience, I reasoned that she probably wouldn't even remember the way I treated her. So why go through with this fruitless exercise. After all, many times old people have a tendency toward being very forgetful. Certainly my mother, reaching the ripe old age of around forty-five would have long forgotten my offenses.

That last gasp at saving face did not work.

I went.

She remembered.

She forgave me.

Did she apologize?

What do you think?

Of course not!

The Lord certainly had much more work to do with her!

Or was it me that He was targeting?

Ephesians 6:2-3, "Honor your father and mother" (this is the first commandment with a promise), "that it may go well with you and that you may live long in the land."

That word "honor", in Greek, is an interesting word. "Timao" means to prize; to fix a valuation on something or someone; to estimate; to fix a value. As the years passed and I learned what the word "honor" actually meant, I realized something. Grocers and other businessmen fix or assign a value to their products which are for sale. If you feel it is reasonably priced, you will purchase it and make it your own.

I had fixed a value (honor) to my mother. She was worth about $.05 to me. You can say, "Brian, how terrible". Yep. But if I want to be honest, that's where my heart was. I had so devalued my mother because of perceived injustices that her net worth to my heart and existence wasn't much. I honored her. I prized her. I fixed a value on her being in my life. It just wasn't a very high value. I didn't need the fingernails-on-the-chalkboard grief of a continued relationship. My young family and I lived four hours away from mom and dad. That was close enough. See them for a couple of days at Christmas, Easter, and summer break. That's enough. After all, one can only hold their breath for so long when visiting someone with whom you'd rather not hang out.

God is relentless. When He invites us to love our neighbor, to honor our mom and dad, He means it. Why? "That it may go well with YOU." He knows the path to true F-R-E-E-D-O-M. He is the way to that freedom. He longs for our hearts to know what He knows because it is who He is love. If we know true love, we know Him. If we know Him, we have been awakened to true love.

There's an interesting story tucked away in Acts 13 that has helped me a lot and it might just help you. Paul and Barnabas were just commissioned by their church at Antioch. As they journey from town to town, they wind up in Pisidian Antioch. They were given the opportunity to speak at the local synagogue one Sabbath day. Paul traced the history of Israel from the captivity in Egypt to King David. Transitioning to David's greatest descendant, he then introduced them to Jesus, His ministry and subsequent death and resurrection. Proclaiming Jesus to be the promised Messiah, the people's hearts were pricked. They wanted to hear more and so invited him to share again on the next Sabbath (Acts 13:16-41). Paul obliged.

In Acts 13:44-45, Luke, the writer of the book of Acts, give the following account:

"The next Sabbath nearly the whole city assembled to hear the word of the Lord. But when the Jews saw the crowds, they were filled with jealousy and began contradicting the things spoken by Paul, and were blaspheming."

Jealousy is a powerful emotion. Boyfriends, jealous over their girlfriends, and husbands, jealous over their wives, can do some very harmful things. Just look at what the jealous Pharisees did to Jesus. As these Jews were "contradicting the things spoken by Paul and were blaspheming", we read in the very next verse,

Acts 13:46, "Paul and Barnabas spoke out boldly and said, "It was necessary that the word of God be spoken to you first; since you repudiate it and judge yourselves *unworthy* of eternal life, behold, we are turning to the Gentiles."

There's that word again. Worthy. Only this time it's the negation of the word. And, it's a different Greek word. This time it's the word "axios". Now, before I explain this word, let me introduce you to the word from which it derives, "ago". The Greek word, "ago", means "to lead; to lead by laying hold of or accompanying - thus bringing someone to a point of destiny or a destination". So, where was Paul in his message trying to "lead" them? What was the destination to which Paul desired to accompany them?

The waiting arms of Jesus and Father.

Forgiveness.

Love.

Hope.

Home.

The Greek word, "axios" means "deserving; weighty; weighing as much as another thing; having like value and worth".

What was the Holy Spirit saying through Paul? He was speaking to the hearts of the people, desiring to lead them to the destination of realizing that they were very valuable to God. They had infinite worth in God's eyes. That's why Father sent the Son. He loved the world so much that He gave His only Son for us.

Jesus would say it like this at the end of His high priestly prayer in John 17:25-26.

"O righteous Father, although the world has not known You, yet I have known You; and these have known that You sent Me; and I have made Your name known to them, and will make it known, so that the love with which You loved Me may be in them, and I in them."

What a weighty thought. Jesus' desired destination for His disciples was to intimately and experientially know the same love of the Father which Jesus had living in Him. He desires for us to also experience this supernatural love… daily… moment-by-moment… forever. Amazing! Humbling. That the greatest love in the universe, the Father's tender heart of mercy, compassion and agape love, can be imparted to our very lives. Did you know you are very valuable to God? He created you. He loves you dearly. You are worthy of His great love.

So what was the response of some of the Jews listening to Paul that day? "...You repudiate it and judge yourselves **unworthy** of eternal life..."

Let's break that down.

First, they "repudiated it". That means they "pushed it off; repelled it; rejected it; to thrust away or drive something away from oneself". That's what the Greek word, "apotheo" means.

Secondly, they "judged themselves". Did you catch that? Some people I've met have a difficult time understanding how a God of love could possibly send someone to hell. My response? He doesn't. You do. When you stand before God on that judgment day, He is simply agreeing with the decision **you made** on earth. You "judged yourself". He loves you so much, He will not violate your free will.

On another level, what did they repudiate? Mercy. Forgiveness. Love. In essence, they rejected and drove away from themselves the sacrifice of Jesus on the cross. He shed His own blood which bought our redemption, thus they rejected the love of the Father being imparted to their hearts. Picture Father reaching His arms out, desperately wanting you to run into those arms of forgiveness and love, and you stubbornly run the other way. We judge ourselves.

Why? Well, Paul answers that also. "...You repudiate it and judge yourselves unworthy of eternal life..." We judge ourselves **unworthy**. We feel we are not worthwhile. Not valuable. Many people live lives of oppression and depression, the enemy eating their lunch day after day. Unworthiness is written all over their faces. Zero value is played out in their lives because what you believe in your heart will manifest to those around you.

Others may put up a good front: arrogant, proud, God's gift to this earth. You probably know a person that puts up that type of appearance. But the reality is, the deception in which our sinful nature exists is so deep and strong, even in our potential outward arrogance, we truly believe that we have very little value and so we are not worthwhile for a God, if He exists, to even care for us, let alone love us enough to die for us.

Do you see why the gospel is the gospel? It is **good news**. It's great news!! It speaks of an infinite God whose final, unchangeable word over our lives is: VALUABLE!! WORTHY!! And so that the enemy of doubt would be silenced once and for all - forever - He sent His Son to prove it.

"Greater love has no one than this that one lay down his life for his friends." (John 15:13)

Many at Pisidian Antioch that day heard Paul speak. Many rejoiced. Many others "judged themselves unworthy of eternal life".

My friend, in which camp do you reside?

God loves you deeply and He will never change His mind about you. HE **IS** LOVE!!

You are worthy of such a great love.

"But as many as received Him, to them He gave the right to become children of God…" (John 1:12)

Allow me to finish this chapter with this testimony. About two or three years ago, I was experiencing tremendous back pain. Getting out of bed was difficult. I would roll out of bed, ease myself onto the floor, and while on hands and knees grab the night stand or push against the wall trying to find the balance between pain and leg strength in order to stand.

While sitting in a chair, I would try a few times to exert enough arm energy and momentum to get myself into a standing position. When successful, my body would be bent at a 90 degree angle at the waist. The next step was to work through the pain in order to stand fully erect. I was in my early 60's.

My son, Daniel, and his wife Treasure, had been at a Bible school on the west coast for a few years while I was experiencing this pain. Upon completion of their Bible training, they came home. It was so good to see them and visit with them.

In the midst of our conversation, Daniel must have noticed my back issues. He asked if he and Treasure could pray for me. He believed God wanted to heal me. I consented. After their prayer, Daniel asked me to get out of my chair to see what God had done. I muscled myself up into my usual 90 degree position and eventually willed myself fully erect. It was obvious I had not been healed. What transpired next I type through tears.

Daniel asked me to sit back down and offered to pray for me one more time. I can't fully explain to you all the thoughts that randomly, hurriedly ran through my mind as I sat back down. Things like, "You will never be healed; you will always be like this; you are not worthy to be healed; Jesus does not want to heal you; you are such a sinner; you are like this because of unrepentant sin in your life; of course Mary (my wife…remember chapter 2?) was healed of arthritis, but that is because she's… Mary… and you are just… Brian… you are not worthy… you are not worthy… you are not worthy… you are not valued by God."

As these thoughts randomly came into my mind in a split second, this is what I heard come out of my mouth, "No Daniel. You don't need to pray for me again. I'm fine. I can live this way. I've lived this way for a while now. I'm getting used to it. I'm fine. I'll be alright."

My son persisted. Reluctantly, I agreed. As He prayed, the Holy Spirit gave me the grace to realize I was repudiating His overtures to my heart. I was like those individuals in Acts 13, though I was a Christian and they were not. I was stiff-arming the Holy Spirit, rejecting the grace He desired to extend to me. Why? God revealed to me in that moment that I actually believed what the thoughts rambling through my mind were telling me, that I was unworthy of receiving this great gift of healing which He wanted to impart to me.

I repented. By His great mercy, He extended grace to me to help me change my mind about how I viewed God. And how I thought He viewed me.

I **was** worthy.

I **was** valuable.

Me. Even me.

Daniel's prayer was short. Next thing I knew I was standing… perfectly erect. There was no pain, but I was weeping. God even loved me!!!

I knew His love, but never like that.

My friend, God loves you. You are a priceless treasure to Him. You are of infinite worth and value to Him. Rejoice!!!

By the way, remember how much I valued my mom when I was younger? About $.05.

My mom died in late April of 2021.

I loved her…dearly.

It was a journey.

A long one.

It was worth it.

My final valuation on my mom: priceless.

That's a much greater honor (value) I gave to her than when I was 25.

Isn't God amazing?

"For this reason I bow my knees before the Father, from whom every family in heaven and on earth derives its name, that He would grant you, according to the riches of His glory, to be strengthened with power through His Spirit in the inner man, so that Christ may dwell in your

hearts through faith; *and* that you, being rooted and grounded in love, may be able to comprehend with all the saints what is the breadth and length and height and depth, and to know the love of Christ which surpasses knowledge, that you may be filled up to all the fullness of God." (Ephesians 3:14-19)

Chapter 10

Did you ever collect baseball cards when you were a kid? I did. Football cards and basketball cards too. It was fun. I had shoe boxes full of them. Looking back, I realize now that God did not give me the gift of a good head for business. Understanding how much collector cards go for these days, if He had put any business savvy in me I'd have saved them with care and probably be a millionaire today. But I was too busy pinning those cards with clothespins to the spokes of my bicycle and riding around the neighborhood making cool noises. Tdddddddddd…it was such an annoying sound! I guess I loved being an annoying little brother. Oh well, so much for being a millionaire via baseball cards.

My dad was into the cards too. Not so much the collecting aspect of it. He was more into shelling out the money for them so I could collect them. I appreciated that. He would take me to the Woolworth or K-Mart stores once a month or so and let me purchase a couple of packs. It was always exciting to quickly open them up to see if I had purchased any cards from my favorite team or favorite players. I always looked forward to doing that with my dad.

I loved my dad. He was an interesting man. He worked hard as an optician his whole life. He was very good at it. One of the best, I think. He loved his family, church work, horse shoes and bowling. He was kind of quiet. Maybe I got that gene from him (if that's inherited). I remember when I was in eighth grade, the optical company he worked for wanted to move him to another city about 90 miles from where we were. The company was downsizing and they felt he had a better chance of staying with them if he moved. Evidently, they were targeting the branch at which he worked for closure. He refused to move. Why? He knew it would be traumatic for us. Our roots were in that city. Home, school, church, friends. He knew how much all of these things meant to my mom, my sister and me. He could not, he would not uproot us from that. I appreciated that about my dad also.

Isn't it interesting what you remember about your parents? As it turns out, the thing I most remember about my dad was his temper. I didn't realize it as a kid, but there was a life lesson in it for me…and him. It would take about 35-40 years to learn it. Let me explain.

Dad had a pretty volatile temper. Yelling. Screaming. It didn't happen too often. But when it did, it was kind of scary. I mean, I was just a little kid. Luckily, it was never directed toward me. My mom got the brunt of it. If you remember from the previous chapter, my mom got the brunt of an awful lot of volcanic activity in our home. To this day I'm not totally certain why that was.

Just as He did with mom, so God did with my dad. When I became an adult, He requested that I talk to dad about the way he was when I was a kid. Just as with mom, I told God, "No".

Same old excuses. He's the (older) adult. He's the dad. I'm the kid (albeit grown up now). He's the one who should initiate this difficult conversation. Again the thought came, what if he never initiated? Would there ever be reconciliation? Would there ever be healing?

Actually, the more I thought about it, the more I realized that my dad had changed over the years. He had mellowed. I hadn't heard that angry tone of voice for quite a while. Maybe I didn't need to bring it up at all. It was over. Yes, that's it. It's a thing of the past. Deal with the past on your own. Let bygones be bygones. Live your life for the here and now. Don't muddy the present and the future with a past that wasn't terrible, just had a few rough patches, even though it hadn't yet been reconciled.

Isn't it interesting how we can play mind games with ourselves? We can as easily talk ourselves out of something as talk ourselves into something…and in the meantime drive ourselves crazy with this incessant rambling in our head. It's called doubt. Being double-minded.

I remember when I was in my mid-30's, God gave me a lesson on doubt that I will never forget. The church my family was attending at the time participated in an Easter drama called The Resurrection Celebration. It was powerful. Five different churches put their denominational differences aside for a season and united their hearts to reach out to the community with this drama. It was written, produced, and directed by a friend of ours who attended our church, and a pastor from a different congregation. They rented the local movie theater for several nights and packed out the place every night. It was thrilling.

Anyway, one year this director-friend of ours asked me to play the role of Jesus. I was flattered, but instead of immediately agreeing, I told her I really needed to pray about it first. See, the Lord had trained me to always inquire of Him first before agreeing to do something. I had been deeply convicted that that's what David had done on a few occasions before he became King of Israel. (See I Samuel 23:2, I Samuel 30:8)

So, that first morning, I went to my quiet place and inquired of the Lord if I should take on this role or not. I heard in my heart a firm "yes". I determined to tell my director-friend that day that I would take the part. The problem was, I didn't see her that day. Usually we would frequently run into each other because the school in which I taught rented the church building where she worked. Well, not a big deal, I thought. I'll just talk to her tomorrow.

The next morning, upon getting out of bed, I went to my quiet place, and for some reason decided that I would inquire about this topic one more time. I wasn't totally comfortable with the "yes" I had received the day before for varying reasons that I'll explain later. This time, however, I heard a "no" in my heart. That, as you can well imagine, was rather confusing. Day 1: yes. Day 2: no. Hmmm. What to do with that? I went to school and avoided my friend. That's what I decided to do with that.

But I had a deadline. She needed an answer very soon because the season for the drama was approaching and she needed to know who was going to comprise her cast. So, I decided on the third morning to inquire of the Lord one more time and see what He would say.

While sitting before the Lord, I heard the Holy Spirit say, "Read James 1". I didn't want to. I told the Lord that I knew what James 1 said. I had just taught it at a men's group a week or two before (as if He didn't know that). Give me something else, I insisted. He persisted. "Read James 1."

And so I reluctantly did. I got to verse 2 of James 1, "Consider it all joy, my brethren, when you encounter various trials…" The Holy Spirit arrested my reading. He asked me what I thought "various trials" meant. I thought for a moment. Getting a diagnosis of cancer, having a heart attack, being involved in a serious car accident…those are "various trials" to me. He agreed with me and then asked if what I was now going through could be considered a "various trial". I knew the correct answer was "yes" but I wasn't feeling it, to be quite honest. But understanding what the word "various" means and knowing a synonym for "trial" is "test", I again, very reluctantly, said "yes". The last two mornings had certainly put me to the test. At this point I was very curious as to where this was going. What was God desiring to teach me? It was certainly challenging what I thought I knew in my head.

The Holy Spirit encouraged me to keep reading. I obliged. When I got to verse five, I knew the Rabbi was about to teach this teacher.

James 1:5, "But if any of you lacks wisdom, let him ask of God, who gives to all generously and without reproach, and it will be given to you."

If I had any doubt before, I now knew that this conversation going on in my head was God-initiated. I was excited. After all, the main reason I inquired of the Lord in the first place was because I "lacked wisdom". I was not interested in doing something on my own initiative. I wanted to know that this was God calling me to take the role in this drama. I was so glad to read the words that God "gives (wisdom) to all generously and without reproach" because I really felt like I needed a good scolding by then. I felt like I deserved reproach from God. In my human-ness, I thought He should say, "I told you once what to do. Why are you coming back to me again and again?"

Isn't it amazing that God does not scold us? He knows and understands our weaknesses. He is very patient with us and a very, very good Teacher.

Well, the next verses explained to me why I was having great difficulties and thus approaching God with the same question for the third morning in a row.

James 1:6-8, "But he must ask in faith without any doubting, for the one who doubts is like the surf of the sea, driven and tossed by the wind. For that man ought not to expect that he will receive anything from the Lord, *being* a double-minded man, unstable in all his ways."

I now understood what the problem was. I was doubting the answer that God had given me. I was exactly like the surf of the sea, driven and tossed by the wind, rising and then falling, rising and then falling. Excited and then deflated. Excited and then deflated. I was double-minded and unstable. How in the world can a person exist healthily when they have a "yes" **and** a "no" tugging at their heartstrings on a very important, potentially life-changing decision they are trying to make? I'm not into weighing pros and cons and going with the one which is the weightiest. The Lord trained me to hear a clear word from Him and then obey, no matter how many cons lined up against that decision. I knew He would take care of the consequences of my obedience. He simply always asked me to obey the leadings of His Holy Spirit.

The problem I now faced was which answer was His leading? "Yes" from Day 1 or "no" from Day 2? Both seemed quite convincing. But I knew doubt was an enemy of faith. So, I needed to know how to proceed. If only I knew how to get rid of the double-mindedness and the confusion it brought.

How God, do I get rid of this double-mindedness?

How do I get rid of this confusion?

"Repent," is what I clearly heard.

I did.

My friend, do you know what it's like to have the slate of your heart wiped clean? Sometimes that slate has a lot of scribble marks drawn on it, none of which make any sense. It can be paralyzing, even when you truly want to do the right thing, the God-pleasing thing. Jesus' blood is powerful. It can truly wipe the slate clean.

I felt free. I was so grateful. But that's only the first step. John 16:8-11 says that the Holy Spirit doesn't just come to convict us of sin, but He also comes to convict us of righteousness. Now that I had a clean slate I needed to persevere and finish this thing. I needed to get an answer as to whether God wanted me to take that role or not. In other words, what was His "right thing" for me to do?

Before I inquired of the Lord one more time, I promised God that I would do exactly what He told me. No more doubt. No more surf of the sea being tossed about, no more double-mindedness. If He said "yes" I would do it. If He said "no" I would decline.

"God, should I consent to this role of portraying the Messiah?"

"Yes."

I saw my director-friend that day and told her I would take the role. She was delighted. So was I, but for different reasons. I had just learned part of a very valuable lesson.

The other part?

Did I tell you the Lord is a very good teacher? Well,

He wanted to debrief with me. The test, the lesson, was not over. He asked me if I wanted to know what was going on behind the scenes during those three days of inquiring followed by doubt, confusion, and frustration. I said, "Yes, I want to know." He reminded me that "God is not the author of confusion, but of peace…" (I Corinthians 14:33). I guess that means that Satan is the author of confusion. But how did he gain access? That was my question.

The Lord took me back to the seeds of doubt that had been planted in my mind after I was unable to give my "yes" to my director-friend on that first day. See, I was a high school teacher. But for the first time in my life, I was teaching grade school. I was teaching in a setting that was a throwback to the old one-room classroom days; a start-up school which a number of Christian families in our congregation had started, asking me to come onboard as the sole teacher. I had 19 students in grades 2-8. That meant I had a lot of preparation to do every day. For grade two there was Bible, reading, grammar, spelling, history, science, and arithmetic. That's seven preps. Remember, we had seven classes (grades 2-8). That amounts to almost 50 preps per day. That doesn't count the corrections that needed to be completed each day for the assignments given. Nor does it count the recess duty. Now, in all fairness, I had a lot of help from moms and dads, but the brunt of the work fell on me.

On top of that, I needed to attend school board meetings as the sole teacher/principal of the school.

On top of that, I was an elder in our church. I needed to attend elder meetings frequently as well as be involved in various other aspects of church life.

On top of that, upon receiving a copy of the drama script, I realized that this Jesus character had a pretty big

role in an Easter drama. I mean, some of the lines I needed
to memorize in this two-hour drama went on for one full page
to a page-and-a-half. And there were several of these
discourses. (Have you read the Sermon on the Mount lately?
It wasn't that long, but you get the idea.)

On top of that, I had a wife whom I loved dearly and
with whom I wanted to spend time.

On top of that, we had four little children at the time
that needed their father's attention.

At the end of Day 1, I began contemplating those
things. Do you see how Satan weaseled into my thoughts at
the end of Day 1? Do you see why doubt was planted in my
mind by the morning of Day 2? And what answer did I get on
Day 2, with all those doubts circulating in my mind? "No."

Thank God for Day 3. By His blood and power there
is resurrection for our lives. No more debilitating, paralyzing
doubt. No more frustration. Just a clear word from God can
set the captive free, whether you're a believer or unbeliever.
We all have "various trials".

By the way, in case you're wondering, I got all the
lines memorized. The drama was very powerful, AND…
school went great and my marriage and family life did not
suffer. Only God could do that!!!

Anyway, back to Dad. I refused to obey the
promptings of the Holy Spirit to talk to my father for literally
years. My reasoning, however, was not because I doubted
that I was hearing correctly. The real excuse was I was
afraid to bring this up to Dad. Would he get angry again?
Would he deny it? Would he say that it wasn't that big of a
deal? Would he mitigate the effects his volatile temper had

on me, my sister, and my mom? Not knowing the answers to all of those questions left me paralyzed. I mean, if it was guaranteed that everything would turn out perfectly, Dad would acknowledge his wrongdoing, he would apologize, I would forgive him, blah, blah, blah; I would probably have approached him…maybe. You see, doubt is not the only weapon the enemy uses to paralyze us from doing God's will. Fear can do the same job.

I remember it well. We were living in Illinois at the time. Mom and Dad had come down from Wisconsin for a weekend visit. I got up early that Sunday morning to be with the Lord as was my custom, and as we visited, He approached me for the umpteenth time to talk to Dad. I wasn't comfortable at all with it…again.

Then, something different happened. This is the only way I can describe it to you. During my time with the Lord, it was as if an invisible scroll came down and rested before my spiritual eyes. On it was something like bullet points: say this, then that, then this, then that. It was brilliant. It was not offensive…which was good. I did not want to offend Dad by bringing these things up from twenty-five or thirty years ago. It was very logical. It made perfect sense. And it had a way to open the conversation and a way to bring the conversation to an appropriate conclusion. All I could think was, "I can do that!"

All fear vanquished. I heard Mom and Dad upstairs in the kitchen fixing some breakfast before they would drive back to Wisconsin. I resolved to take the script that had been implanted in my heart and speak to my father.

"Dad, do you remember when I was a kid that you had a pretty bad temper?"

"Yes."

"Do you know how that affected me?"

"No."

"Well, I love you a lot, Dad. But, when you became angry and started yelling and screaming, I was quite afraid of you."

"Really? No, I didn't know that."

"Dad, it wouldn't have been so bad if you would have said one thing to me during those years. That one thing would have made everything so much better."

"Oh really? I didn't know that either."

"Dad, do you know what that one thing was that you could have said to me to make it all better?"

"No, what Son?"

"You could have said, 'Brian, I'm so sorry for yelling and screaming around the house.' But I never heard those words come out of your mouth. Not once did you apologize for your temper tantrums."

The next thing that came out of my father's mouth knocked me off balance. I didn't see it coming, but it was extremely revealing. "Brian, I thought about apologizing for my behavior many times, but I didn't because I thought it would undermine my authority in the house."

I was stunned. I then heard these loving, compassionate words come out of my mouth: "Dad, apologizing for bringing fear through an out-of-control temper would not have **undermined** your authority, it would have **established** your authority in the home."

I went on to explain to my dad that we all sin, we all make mistakes. But the way to bring healing to our relationships when we make mistakes is by owning them and apologizing for them to the individuals that were affected by them.

My dad looked me in the eye and said, "Brian, I am so sorry for the way I acted when you were younger."

"Dad, I forgive you."

Dad was not a hugger.

We embraced.

He initiated.

He would not let me go for the longest time.

A mountain was lifted off my heart…and probably his.

That's my dad. I love him. He went to be with the Lord in 2013. He was a changed man from when I was a kid. It wasn't age that changed him. It wasn't that he mellowed as he grew older. Jesus got ahold of his heart.

I miss him.

One day, I'll see him again and we'll continue that hug. The only difference will be that the invisible Jesus that joined in the hug that day long ago will visibly join in the hug on that day in the future.

And maybe, just maybe, together we'll go and talk to some of our sports heroes who made it to heaven who were on those baseball, football, and basketball cards.

That would be fun.

<u>Chapter 11</u>

I enjoy sports. I have many memories from my growing up years related to sports. Like the many times I'd watch the Green Bay Packers on television on a Sunday afternoon and then at half time, my friend and I would go outside and try to kick field goals through the branched tree trunk in the vacant field next to my parents' house.

In the summer, we'd make a rectangle out of masking tape on the garage door, simulating a strike zone. We would then take turns pitching like we were the next Cy Young award winner while the other would bat, dreaming of one day being the next Mickey Mantle.

But basketball was my favorite. I enjoyed shooting from outside the lane. Given my slight frame, it was easier shooting from out there than being closer to the hoop where all the physical banging and shoving went on. My favorite player was Brian Winters. Loved his first name. Plus, he was a terrific shooter from the outside. My friends even called me "Winters" when I would "let it fly".

I also loved the biblical character King David. Not sure why. Maybe it was his underdog status. Runt of the family. Forgotten. Overlooked. Oppressed. Constantly running and hiding in caves. Maybe he reminded me of my favorite sports teams (after the Vince Lombardi era for the Packers; after the Kareem Abdul Jabbar era for the Milwaukee Bucks; after the Robin Yount era for the Milwaukee Brewers): all underdogs. Maybe he reminded me of how I often felt. Tremendous oppression seemed to be my constant companion.

David's Psalms were my constant diet.

"I'm crying out to You, God."

"Are you there?"

"When will this oppression ever end?"

"When will You crush my (invisible) enemies?"

"Help me, O God."

"I will ever praise You, my King and my God."

They offered me perspective. Sometimes we are encouraged to keep going through hard times when we realize we're not alone in our difficulties. As I read about David's story and his Psalms, I realized that through it all, he was victorious because he always kept his eyes on His God, who happened to be my God as well. David was raw. He was brutally honest with God concerning his life; the good, bad, and ugly. I liked that. He talked to God as if God was actually his friend. I *really* liked that.

I especially liked the passage that stated that David was a "man after His (God's) own heart," (I Samuel 13:14, Acts 13:22). That's what I wanted. I wanted to grow up to be a man panting after God like a deer pants for the water streams. I wanted to be a man that God could promote if He so chose. I wanted to be a man totally in love with Jesus. I wanted to be like David.

Then when I got older and started a family with my wife, we went to a conference together. After his message, the speaker began ministering to the five hundred or more people who had gathered. The Lord highlighted about ten to fifteen people to whom he should minister. Guess who one of those people was? Guess what this total stranger said to me? That's right. He said I would one day be the next Green Bay Packer great. Well, not exactly. That probably wasn't going to happen at 125 pounds…soaking wet. He looked into my eyes and told me God had planted in me a heart like King David. I was a man after God's own heart.

I flew out of the auditorium that day (not literally). I was both humbled and excited, broken and built up. God knew me! He saw me! He understood my pain. He felt my suffering. He loved me. He had a plan for me.

Less than a year later I had my dream job. I would be a full-time minister. I was sooo excited.

Six years later, I resigned. Broken. Confused. More oppressed than ever.

Another six years later, The Lord asked me if I wanted to know what that first six years was all about. Why had the dream of my life turned into a nightmare? From His perspective, what happened?

You know, if we live our lives from our narrow, temporal, transient perspective all the time, we will miss the big picture of what God has been doing all along. If we miss His perspective, then we are doomed to a life, or at least a season of our life, that is marked by much less than the *abundant* life our Creator promised us.

I told Him "yes", I wanted Him to show me what that first six years was all about.

He told me to read the Book of Jude.

I did.

I understood nothing…until I got to verse 11.
"Woe to them! For they have gone the way of Cain, and for pay they have rushed headlong into the error of Balaam, and perished in the rebellion of Korah."

I asked the Holy Spirit why He was illuminating this particular verse. I mean, I was like David. Remember? Man after God's own heart?

"Because you have been acting just like Cain, Balaam, and Korah."

Talk about the walls going up. I did not want any part of this conversation. I'm a David. Remember? Good. Anything else before I walk away from this conversation?

The Holy Spirit persisted. He took me back twelve, thirteen, fourteen years. He reminded me of interactions I had with people. He showed me that He had put people in my life to encourage me to say no to my selfish ambitions. I would not listen. Like Balaam.

He showed me that when I finally became a minister of the Gospel of Jesus Christ, I was just like Cain. I was not my brother's keeper. I only wanted to use people for my selfish, ambitious purposes, namely, being the next great preacher of the Word of God. I wanted to build my own kingdom, not His.

He showed me that this selfish ambition which had gripped my heart tempted me to be like Korah, bad-mouthing the leaders placed in my life, just as Korah had done to Moses. I was trying to advance my cause, my ministry, my kingdom, by making other leaders look inferior to me.

Like Jonah in the belly of the fish, He had my full attention. He would not let me go until I saw everything He saw and knew what He knew about the last 14 years of my life. I gained His perspective seated with Him in the heavenlies as he mercifully flashed those years before my consciousness.

I wept.

I was broken.

I repented.

Another "man after God's heart", after great personal failure, once wrote, "Hide Your face from my sins and blot out all my iniquities. Create in me a clean heart, O God, and renew a steadfast spirit within me. Do not cast me away from Your presence and do not take Your Holy Spirit from me," (Psalm 51:9-11).

That became my prayer. I'm so grateful that He is in the business of healing the brokenhearted and that He does not despise a broken and contrite heart. (See Isaiah 61:1, Psalm 51:17)

Why am I telling you all of this? Because I wanted you to know the context of one of the greatest desires I've ever had. See, it was during those first six years when I was acting like Cain, Balaam, and Korah that something else was being deposited in my heart. I called it the Renaissance Center. I desired to build a spiritual Center of continual praise and worship to my God. That would form the foundation of the ministry. One pillar of this Center would be discipleship, where students would come for sound Biblical teaching *and* be encouraged one-on-one. Drama and theater, painting and drawing, writing, journaling…in other words, a total release of the arts would be another pillar of the Center. It would have a coffee house/restaurant for people to come and fellowship; a place where the hungry were fed physically and spiritually. There would be a place where kids could come and be kids while playing games and enjoying fellowship with each other and with the Holy Spirit.

This was my greatest dream, birthed during those first six years. However, at the end of those six years and for many years following, I became so disillusioned, so disappointed, so out of sorts, that I began embracing the thought that the Renaissance Center was an Ishmael. I had, in my own imagination, birthed an Ishmael. Trust me, if you're a man or woman after God's heart, the last thing you want to do is birth an Ishmael.

If you're not sure what I'm talking about, Ishmael was Abraham's son born of Hagar. Hagar was the handmaiden or servant of Sarah, Abraham's wife. That story (Genesis chapters 16-18) did not start well and did not end well. We are still seeing the consequences on the earth from that poorly conceived (pun intended) decision. That's what happens when we do things according to the whims of our own sinful flesh instead of the Spirit of God.

The thought of desiring to birth an Ishmael tormented me more than anything for the next decade or more. I became super careful about any dreams or visions about advancing God's kingdom that came into my head. In fact, I was afraid to dream or envision anything anymore. That's pretty tough when you love being a visionary of sorts. This started in 1999.

Let me take you to 2021. My pastor back in 1999 eventually left our church to plant a church in Indiana, where he stayed for several years. He then pastored another church in Iowa for several more. Then, God sent him back to our church in 2020. I began meeting with him and one of my sons in April of 2021. Being a man who asks tremendous questions and has wonderful insight, he began asking me what I'd been doing for the last 20 years and what I had in my heart. I shared with him everything I have just disclosed to you. Upon hearing of my "Ishmael", he thoughtfully looked at me and said, "Brian, I'm not sure the Renaissance Center was an Ishmael at all. I'm wondering if it was a miscarriage."

I don't think I can adequately explain to you what that said to me. In my mind, Ishmael spells intentional or unintentional wrongdoing bringing guilt, condemnation, and shame, all of which I had carried for many years. I mean, I wanted to build God's kingdom. I just didn't realize I was doing it my way, not His.

"Unless the Lord builds the house they labor in vain who build it," (Psalm 127:1).

Miscarriage does not have that connotation, at least in my mind. A miscarriage is a terribly unfortunate happening. Something out of our control. Extremely sad but not necessarily something that would carry the weight of guilt, condemnation, and shame over wrongdoing, like an Ishmael.

I certainly had something to pray about. I needed to discern whether the Renaissance Center was an Ishmael or a miscarriage. The ramifications of the two were immensely different.

The next morning, I went to my quiet place to seek the Lord. I heard Him say a very strange thing. "This morning, you are going to need to mourn."

I thought that to be strange. I wasn't about to manufacture tears. I probably could, but I wasn't into acting in the presence of the Lord. I'd rather be real. So I wondered what He meant.

Then something happened that's very difficult to describe. I began sensing the Lord's presence very strongly. As I did, I also sensed there was someone with Him. Slowly, I began to understand who it was. You see, between our fourth and fifth child, my wife and I miscarried a child. That child was now standing with Jesus right before me in this experience He was so graciously granting me. (I call our miscarried baby, "child", because the gender was not revealed to me in this experience.)

My breathing became labored. It was like I was dreaming but I was wide awake.

Then the child spoke to me.

"It's nice up here, Daddy."

I began weeping.

"I love you, Daddy."

I was now sobbing.

"Daddy, I'm alive!"

I totally broke. Holding a pillow to my face so I would not wake up my wife, I sobbed and sobbed uncontrollably for several minutes. God was right. It would be a morning of mourning.

Then the experience was over.

Apart from the thrilling, heart-wrenching, gracious encounter with my child, I knew instantly what the Lord was speaking to me. The Renaissance Center, which was birthed over twenty years prior in my heart, was **not** an Ishmael after all. It had miscarried over the years. But just as our child was a seed planted in my wife's womb and lives on throughout eternity, so The Renaissance Center was a seed planted in my heart long ago and was still alive. Why? Because **Jesus** is alive. **He** is the resurrection and the life. He planted that seed. It was not from my sinful, fleshly imagination.

My pastor, Lynn Furrow, my son Joseph, and I have continued meeting since that experience in April of 2021.

The Renaissance Center, now named Adoration School of Ministry, humbly opened in September of 2022.

I am broken.

I am busy.

I am grateful.

I believe that God wants to impact thousands upon thousands and more with His beautiful love.

Renaissance, revival, rebirth is upon us.

I will live to see it.

I'm excited.

I'm so grateful he made me a man after His heart.

I'm even more grateful He is a God after my heart.

He's after your heart too.

Open your heart to Him and see what miraculous things He will do.

The bowl of popcorn with your name on it may have been hidden by your loving Heavenly Father, but he waits in excitement for you to find it. What are you waiting for?

www.ingramcontent.com/pod-product-compliance
Lightning Source LLC
Chambersburg PA
CBHW051444150726
48000CB00005B/2245